Effective Classroom Management

Management

Six Keys to Success

DIANNE F. BRADLEY
JUDITH ANN PAULEY
JOSEPH F. PAULEY

ROWMAN & LITTLEFIELD EDUCATION
Lanham, Maryland • Toronto • Oxford
2006

Published in the United States of America
by Rowman & Littlefield Education
A Division of Rowman & Littlefield Publishers, Inc.
A wholly owned subsidary of The Rowman & Littlefield Publishing Group, Inc.
4501 Forbes Boulevard, Suite 200, Lanham, Maryland 20706
www.rowmaneducation.com

PO Box 317
Oxford
OX2 9RU, UK

British Library Cataloguing in Publication Information Available

Library of Congress Cataloging-in-Publication Data

Bradley, Dianne F., 1944–
    Effective classroom management : six keys to success / Dianne F. Bradley, Judith Ann
Pauley, Joseph F. Pauley.
        p. cm.
    Includes bibliographical references and index.
    ISBN-13: 978-1-57886-302-0 (pbk. : alk. paper)
    ISBN-10: 1-57886-302-3 (pbk. : alk. paper)
    1. Classroom management.   I. Pauley, Judith A.   II. Pauley, Joseph F.   III. Title.

LB3013.B655 2006
371.102'4—dc22   2005018856

♾ ™ The paper used in this publication meets the minimum requirements of
American National Standard for Information Sciences—Permanence of
Paper for Printed Library Materials, ANSI/NISO Z39.48-1992.
Manufactured in the United States of America.

To all the teachers who are using the concepts of
Process Communication in their classrooms
to make a difference in their students' lives.

Contents

Foreword

Are you a student teacher about to begin that exciting challenge of going solo for the first time? Are you, after teaching for three to five years, now raising questions about being a career teacher? Are you a veteran educator who continues to search for more effective educational theories and practices? It is likely that, although you have translated your hard-earned content knowledge into many exciting lesson plans, you know that your classroom skills could be enhanced with more effective approaches to classroom management. In the book *Six Keys to Successful Classroom Management*, Bradley, Pauley, and Pauley describe exciting new research-based actions you can take by applying teacher-tested principles and practices of the Process Communication Model (PCM).

As a professor of special education at several major universities, I have devoted more than thirty years to researching effective teaching and learning practices to accelerate the academic and social learning of students with special needs. Currently I hold the title of professor emeritus at Arizona State University, and I am a visiting professor at Florida International University, where I teach advanced graduate students in school psychology and special education. I have met a wide range of researchers and have learned diverse ways of thinking about teaching, learning, and classroom management. I can use and teach others to use direct instruction, reinforcement theory, creative thinking models, cooperative group learning, multiple intelligence models, computer-assisted instruction, competency- or performance-based assessments, self-regulation and self-determination skills development, collaborative consultation, and co-teaching. Then, in 1997, while on sabbatical at California State University, San Marcos, I worked with Dr. Jacqueline Thousand, who had been applying PCM to her teaching. The results that her graduates obtained were so impressive that I was convinced to apply PCM in my own teaching and research efforts. I then embarked on a series of workshops, classes, and advanced training seminars with the Pauley and Pauley team.

One reason why I am such a strong advocate of the PCM approach to classroom management is that I have seen it work wonders in many diverse areas. I am a much better teacher and researcher as a consequence of applying PCM principles and practices in my own work. My family life has been enriched through the knowledge and skills I have acquired through PCM. Instead of judging my students or family members as wrong or contrary; I seek to energize that part of my personality that can better communicate with them. I have learned to welcome the behaviors of students in distress as a signal for me to change my behaviors toward them. Instead of heaping punishment or admonitions, I can now offer choices for energizing activities and compliments that better meet their psychological needs.

In fact, you may realize, as I do, that *Six Keys to Successful Classroom Management* comes to educators at a crucial time in education. Teachers must not only meet the increasingly diverse academic and social needs of the K–12 students who enter their classrooms but also balance the seemingly incompatible demands for individualization and standardization. In fact, this combination of stressors can lead to burnout, demoralization, and, in some cases, untimely decisions to leave the profession. Rutherford (2004) states that 50 percent of all new teachers leave the profession within their first five years. Some of the reasons for this astonishing statistic have been identified by researchers such as Wood and McCarthy (2002), who summarize the current research and theoretical bases for teacher burnout:

> Given that teachers must face a classroom full of students every day, negotiate potentially stressful interactions with parents, administrators, counselors, and other teachers, contend with relatively low pay and shrinking school budgets, and ensure students meet increasingly strict standards of accountability, it is no wonder many experience a form of burnout at some point in their careers.

You may wonder what the relationship is between teacher burnout and classroom management. Hastings and Bham (2003) studied the classroom behaviors of one hundred teachers. The measures for teacher burnout showed differential prediction by pupil behavior. Pupil disrespect and lack of social skills predicted teacher emotional exhaustion, depersonalization, and personal accomplishment burnout. *Six Keys to Successful Classroom Management* offers a viable alternative to teachers who are tempted to drop out of the profession because of unruly students.

As I have used the PCM keys to classroom management, I find that it is easy for me to listen to my students, keenly observe their actions and interactions, and continuously change my responses to better meet their needs. Imagine a classroom where you gain the active respect of your students and engender more socially acceptable interactions from your students by applying the *Six Keys*. Thanks to the explicit step-by-step procedures described by the authors, you too can create a responsive and effective classroom management system. The research base is clear: you can experience the same results that other teachers obtained when they applied the *Six Keys*. They noted improvements in academic performance and decreases in negative behaviors from students with disabilities, students at risk for school failure, and students from troubled homes.

May your own journey to more effective classroom management using *Six Keys* be as joyful and challenging as mine has been. In closing, I sincerely thank the Bradley, Pauley, and Pauley writing team for their decision to write this book. By sharing their wisdom and the experiences of K–12 classroom teachers who have applied PCM principles and practices, they show their values for listening to students and taking actions to help them succeed.

Ann Nevin, professor emeritus
Arizona State University

REFERENCES

Hastings, R., & Bham, M. (2003). The relationship between student behavior patterns and teacher burnout. *School Psychology International, 24*(1), 115–127. Abstract retrieved January 4, 2005, from http://spi.sagepub.com/cgi/content/abstract/24/1/115

Rutherford, P. (2004). *Why didn't I learn this in college?* Alexandria, VA: Attitudes, Skills, & Knowledge (ASK), Inc.

Wood, T., & McCarthy, C. (2002). Understanding and preventing teacher burnout. ED477726. Retrieved January 4, 2005, from http://www.vtaide.com/png/ERIC/Teacher-Burnout.htm

Acknowledgments

First of all, we want to thank Dr. Taibi Kahler, Ph.D., for his friendship and for the profound impact he has had on our lives and the lives of millions of others. He has encouraged us and cooperated with us every step of the way in helping us write this book. President Bill Clinton called Dr. Kahler a genius for his discoveries in personality theory and for his ability to express them in an easily applied system for understanding and improving interpersonal relationships (W. J. Clinton, personal communication, June 4, 1997). We certainly second President Clinton's assessment. Dr. Kahler has significantly impacted organizations and people through the application of his Process Communication Model® (PCM) to management, psychotherapy, and interpersonal communications. As the success stories in this book clearly demonstrate, the concepts of PCM are equally effective when applied in the classroom. They are especially effective in helping teachers reach and teach the hard-to-reach student.

We have been helping teachers apply the concepts of PCM in their classrooms for many years. The teachers have enthusiastically used the concepts and have been very excited with their successes. Many teachers told us they wish we would write a book on how to apply the concepts to help teachers manage their classes more effectively. This book is our response to them.

We acknowledge Don and Pam Reed, the co-owners of Kahler Communications Atlanta, for their friendship, for their insights into Promoters, and for their help in writing the Promoter dialogues. The dialogues are more realistic because of their input.

We greatly appreciate the talents of Brian Lofgren, who contributed the artwork. His sketches bring to life "Heather" and the six personality types and help make the book more reader friendly.

We are grateful to Dr. Michael Gilbert, Ph.D., professor of educational leadership and chair of the Department of Educational Administration and Community Leadership, Central Michigan University, for his friendship and his willingness to exchange ideas on the application of the concepts of PCM in the classroom. He has also encouraged his students to consider doing their doctoral dissertations on applications of PCM. Several of them have done so. We want to acknowledge them and all those who have done research for their doctoral dissertations or master's theses on the results when the concepts of PCM are applied in the classroom. We have quoted from several of them in this book. Specifically, we want to acknowledge Dr. Rebecca Bailey, Dr. Mark Wallin, Dr. Sue Martin, Dr. Nancy Hawking, and Ms. Ann Shioji. Several more teachers are currently doing research for their dissertations. We are eagerly awaiting the results of their studies.

We also are indebted to all the teachers and other educators who have attended our seminars and who enthusiastically shared with us their experiences in applying the concepts in their classrooms. They made this book possible. All the interventions discussed in this book are real-life examples that were contributed by teachers all over the country who have attended our seminars and applied the concepts of PCM in their classes. Specifically, we wish to thank the following educators for allowing us to use their stories: Cory Anastasi, Jennifer Boone, Camille Brown, Carolyn Brunt, Darlene Deck, Jennifer Gastauer, Sofia Hernandez, Constance Hill, Sarah Lloyd, Barbara Sabatini, Nikole Shaeffer, Mary-Ellyn Tarzy, and Kimberly Emswiler.

Special thanks go to Dr. Ann Nevin, professor emeritus at Arizona State University, for her suggestions for improving the manuscript and for agreeing to write the foreword.

Introduction

The pressure is on! Students, teachers, administrators, and families feel it. High-stakes testing is dominating decision making in schools. Students are being required to meet state standards, putting administration and teaching jobs as well as student promotion on the line. Schools with large numbers of students from low socioeconomic status, high numbers of special education students, and increasing populations of non-English-speaking students are wondering how they can prepare their students to meet these standards. Those in schools who are typically high functioning wonder how they can continue to make "annual yearly progress" and improve test scores each year. The pressure for high student performance has never been greater.

In order to attempt to comply with high-stakes testing mandates, school districts seem to have selected one of two paths to address the preparation of students for the attainment of the prescribed standards. Some have chosen to implement specialized programs, such as structured reading curricula, accompanied by drill and practice on exercises designed as testing simulations. Enhanced homeschool communication, such as informing parents that their children need a good night's sleep and a healthy breakfast on the day of the test, complete the preparation. In order to attempt to help each student reach the standards set forth by the school district, teachers report that they are using strategies they don't really believe support good instructional practices (Pedulla, 2003). These might include workbooks that are set up like test booklets, drill and practice of facts and procedures, and structured, repetitive commercial materials.

However, other schools have realized that in order for students to achieve the designated standards, the focus needs to be on enhancing effective teaching practices. In addition to providing a viable curriculum, giving timely and specific feedback, and involving parents in their children's education, the educational literature identifies several other important factors that lead to successful instruction. These are 1) motivating students to want to be in school and learn, 2) sound classroom management, and 3) the use of effective teaching strategies. Knowledge of the Process Communication Model® (PCM) can enhance these vital areas and help teachers streamline methods that complement all three areas.

This book will take the reader inside the classroom of a well-regarded, experienced teacher who has gathered many tools over the years for classroom and behavior management. She has found that some work with some students, that other tools work with other students, but that none work with all. Each year, there are students she has difficulty motivating, managing, or teaching successfully. Through the unique and dynamic concepts of PCM, she discovers ways to motivate and manage even the types of students who had been behavioral challenges to her in the past. As a bonus, she finds greater satisfaction and fulfillment in her daily interactions with students and a renewed dedication to her teaching career.

Although told as the story of one teacher, this book is a compilation of the experiences of many teachers who have been trained in PCM. They are stories from real teachers all over the country who have used this model successfully with students of all ages and personality types.

PART I

THE SIX KEYS

1

The Perfect Plan

Key 1: Know Yourself

Refreshed from several weeks off and a week at the beach with her family, Heather Thompson felt revitalized, and she was determined that this would be her best school year ever teaching sixth grade. Armed with some new strategies from a summer workshop on classroom management, she was looking forward to applying what she had learned, especially with Randi and JP in her class this year.

Even though school wouldn't officially start for a few days, Heather wanted to be completely ready before the students arrived, so she spent several days preparing her classroom bulletin boards and materials. The workshop she had taken on classroom management had emphasized the importance of structure and routine as well as understandable and visible classroom standards. The first thing she did was draft a list of classroom rules on the computer. She added clip art to make it attractive and had it enlarged and copied so she could hang it in several prominent places in her classroom. She then added attractive posters with motivational sayings on them to complete the decoration of her classroom:

Classroom Rules for Ms. Thompson's Room

1. Enter the room quietly.
2. Sit in your assigned seat.
3. Respect and be kind to others.
4. One person talks at a time.
5. Raise your hand before speaking.
6. Keep your work area neat.

Heather believes that education is the most important component of a person's life and wants to instill this value in the students she teaches. She is dedicated to her job as an educator and believes she can make a difference in the lives of her students. She strives to do her job well, learning as much as she can about each of her students. Her mission is to have each student be the best that he or she can be. Therefore, doing things correctly, neatly and to the best of one's ability is expected in her class. The students she has trouble understanding are the ones who don't seem to care about their grades or their futures.

Because of her own high expectations for herself and the amount of extra work she takes on (committee chairs, team leader, working on her master's degree), Heather sometimes stretches herself too thin and becomes stressed. When this happens, Heather is much more likely to focus on mistakes than on what is done well. She lectures the students on the importance of education and admonishes them to do better in their schoolwork. She gives them advice about what it takes to get good grades and how those grades will affect them in the future. These traits reflect the **Persister** part of her personality, the part that is the strongest (see figure 1.1). Heather is dedicated, observant, and conscientious and has a strong set of values by which she lives and through which she filters her world.

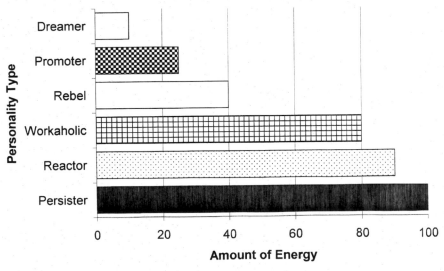

Figure 1.1 Heather's Personality Structure

Heather is also a warm, compassionate person who genuinely cares about all her students as well as her colleagues. She often brings homemade treats for the staff and for her students and takes a personal interest in their lives. Her classroom is tastefully decorated and comfortable with large throw pillows and brightly painted bookshelves in the reading corner. She has a great depth of feeling for people and strives to be liked by the students and staff. Students are frequently reminded about how others feel when they are inconsiderate or mean to each other. The strong **Reactor** part of her personality reflects her sensitivity toward others and her nurturing ways.

Heather also has quite a bit of energy in her **Workaholic** personality part. This is evidenced by her coming to work at school before the required time to make sure she is ready for the students when they arrive. She has made lists of all the things she has to do and has her electronic grade book and attendance

Heather

database prepared well in advance. She has organized her schedule for the first week of school. Heather's well-developed personality parts of Persister, Reactor, and Workaholic are easy for her to access and have helped her successfully prepare for the opening of the school year. According to the research findings of the Process Communication Model® (PCM) developed by Dr. Taibi Kahler, an internationally recognized clinical psychologist, (Kahler, 1982), Heather Thompson is a Persister in a Reactor phase with a strong Workaholic component in her personality. What does this mean, and how will it affect her relationships with the students she is preparing for?

THE SIX BASE PERSONALITIES

Process Communication describes people as being one of six personality types based on how they take in information and perceive the world around them (Pauley, Bradley, & Pauley, 2002). This personality type is known as an individual's base personality. This is the part of their personality that individuals energize the most and determines their preferred communication style. More than 85 percent of teachers have a base personality of Persister, Reactor, or Workaholic (Gilbert, 2004). The character strengths associated with a person's base personality type remain the strongest part of their personality throughout their life. It is believed that people are born with their base personality already established because it is possible to identify the characteristics of a person's base personality type within a few days of their birth and certainly by the time they are two months old.

The six personality types have been labeled Workaholic, Persister, Reactor, Dreamer, Rebel, and Promoter. **Workaholics** are responsible, logical, and organized. They think first and want people to think with them. **Persisters** are conscientious, dedicated, and observant. They get a little information and quickly form an opinion. They want people to respect them for their commitment to ideals. **Reactors** are compassionate, sensitive, and warm. They feel first and want people to feel with them. **Dreamers** are reflective, imaginative, and calm. They are very deliberate and need time to reflect on things before acting. **Rebels** are creative, spontaneous, and playful. They react to the world through their likes and dislikes and like to have people around them who are fun. **Promoters** are resourceful, adaptable, and charming. They are action oriented and act first before thinking. They make things happen and like people around them who are active and exciting.

THE PERSONALITY STRUCTURE

Although everyone has a base personality type, Process Communication incorporates all six types into a person's personality structure. In other words, each person has all six personality types in them to varying degrees. With practice, we can strengthen these types so that we can energize each type whenever we choose.

The order of the personality types in people is established by the time they are seven years old and, other than the base, probably is determined by environmental factors (Kahler, 1996). Each person has a certain amount of energy in each type, resulting in some types being "stronger" than others. Most adults are able to energize two or three of these types fairly easily, but most children may be able to energize only one or two of these types on a regular basis. Therein lies the challenge for teachers.

Most teachers are strong in Persister and Workaholic energy, and many elementary school and special education teachers are often strong in their Reactor as well. In class they tend to teach the way these three types of students learn and manage their classrooms in ways that these three types can relate to. What about the other three types—Dreamers, Rebels, and Promoters? These are the types of students whom most educators have difficulty with, and they often need more strategies to be able to reach them. Before looking at specific examples of ways to manage the classroom to reach all six types of students, let's see what each of these types is like as a teacher.

Persister Teachers

Many teachers are strong in Persister energy and enter the teaching profession because of their deep and committed beliefs to the value of education. Because all events are filtered through their well-established value system and strong beliefs, teachers who are high in Persister energy are often described as dedicated, observant, and conscientious. They dedicate themselves to helping their students be all that they can be and are willing to devote themselves totally to helping students who show a willingness to learn. They may make themselves available to help their students before school, at lunch, after school, or on weekends, frequently adjusting their schedules to accommodate the schedules of their students. Because of their dedication, they are often described as being driven to help their students succeed.

All information that Persisters give and receive has been filtered through their own belief system and is rooted in their opinions. Often they form an opinion based on assumptions. They have strong views about each of their students and teach using pedagogical tools that they believe are most effective. Because the favorite learning and teaching style of Persisters is auditory, they frequently use lecture to teach concepts and impart information. This works well with students who have high Persister or Workaholic energy but frequently results in miscommunication with the other types of students and can contribute to waning interest as well as behavior and classroom management problems.

Persister teachers believe that learning is serious business, that discipline and student safety are essential to promote student learning, and that rules are important in creating an effective learning environment. They support the theory that lessons, like life, have a moral. Therefore, they expect their students to obey rules set by the school and teacher and may grow impatient with students who do not adhere to school and classroom standards or who seem not to care about learning.

It is not important to teachers with high Persister energy that their students like them. However, they do want to be respected by their students and also by their peers for their knowledge of subject matter and for their dedication to teaching. In addition, they like to hear that they are effective teachers and have done a good job helping their students master the material. They take great pride in their students' accomplishments and are thrilled when their students score well on achievement tests. They look on these accomplishments as indicators that their students have applied themselves to learning and have succeeded. They are especially pleased when students return after graduation and thank them for being such a dedicated teacher.

A Persister teacher may:

1. Post classroom rules.

2. Lecture on the value of education.

3. Frequently use "you should . . ."

4. Display motivational posters.

5. Make extra time available to help students.

6. Be driven to help each student succeed.

7. Demonstrate their belief in treating all students fairly.

8. Be actively involved in activities and organizations to improve their teaching.

9. Take leadership roles in something they believe in.

10. Punish students who don't follow the rules.

11. Get angry with students who are not working up to potential.

12. Use sarcasm.

13. Expect perfection in self and others.

14. Demand respect.

Reactor Teachers

Teachers who are high in Reactor energy are sensitive, warm, and compassionate and frequently nurture their students. They filter their environment through their emotions so they "feel" everything that happens. They have excellent people skills and often treat the students in their classrooms like family. They become teachers because they want to help students. It is no surprise that many Reactors pursue elementary and special education.

Reactor teachers like a cozy, peaceful environment and therefore arrange their classrooms so that everyone can feel comfortable. They sometimes set up their rooms in cooperative groups of four or five that function like substitute families. They may bring in cuddly stuffed animals and have plants interspersed around the room. The use of large pillows and carpeted spaces makes the classroom a welcoming place and helps their students be as comfortable as possible. Colorful posters and pictures of happy people may adorn the bulletin boards and walls.

Reactor teachers genuinely like their students, as well as their colleagues, and are most effective teaching when they feel appreciated and liked by their students. They often go out of their way to reach out to the students, their parents, and the other teachers. Because Reactor teachers want everyone to like them, they frequently put off their own desires until after they have taken care of everyone else. They want everyone to get along well, so when people argue or create a disturbance in their class, they may take this personally and internalize that they are doing something wrong. When this happens, they may end up making silly mistakes on things that they really know how to do well, such as misspelling a word in a letter that goes home to parents. This frequently exacerbates the problem and results in additional classroom management problems.

Reactor teachers are most effective when they know their students and their colleagues like them. It is very important for Reactor teachers to have their fellow staff members and even their supervisors spend time talking with them about subjects they are interested in, such as their families, their health, their friends, or their colleagues. Spending this type of time with Reactors is important to them because it reassures them that they are liked and cared about.

Reactor teachers may:

1. Have a warm, cozy, nest-like classroom.
2. Nurture staff and students.
3. Have plants and stuffed animals in the classroom.
4. Engage in personal conversations with staff and students.
5. Have pictures of smiling, happy people decorating their classroom.
6. Provide food for students and staff.
7. Use stickers as rewards.
8. Want students and staff to like them.
9. Have students seated in groups and encourage them to work together.
10. Become upset when there is disharmony in the classroom or school.
11. Make mistakes when upset.

Workaholic Teachers

Responsible, logical, and organized are the words that describe the Workaholic teacher. In today's high-powered schools with a multitude of teacher expectations, high Workaholic energy serves teachers well. Workaholics can multitask and do well with organization and order. They are able to teach concepts in a logical sequence and thrive on having a schedule and a routine. They enjoy taking courses and are usually lifelong learners who enthusiastically put new concepts they have learned into practice. They often have reputations as excellent teachers and hard workers.

Workaholic teachers thrive on being recognized for the good job they are doing. You may find their rooms and offices adorned with plaques, certificates, and awards. They save letters of recognition from parents, administrators, and students. There is no greater reward than running into a student later in life and hearing, "You taught me more than any teacher I ever had!" Workaholics prize positive comments about their work from their supervisors and colleagues, and this further helps them to succeed and do their best. Teachers who have high Workaholic energy respond well to a set routine and usually provide this for their students in the form of a syllabus or daily schedule with time frames. They set up classroom routines so that students know what is expected. Organizational tools such as databases, personal digital assistants, calendars, and time trackers aid them in their organizational schema, and they expect their students to utilize them as well.

To Workaholics, time is of the utmost importance and should be used wisely to accomplish as much as possible. They tend to rely heavily on schedules, so when an unexpected schedule change occurs, it can throw the Workaholic into a chaotic state until the change can be assimilated into a new framework. They have little tolerance for students who do not strive to do their best and get good grades or who do things the teacher considers a waste of time. Students who fool around in class, act silly, are off task, or don't care about their grades are difficult for a Workaholic teacher to understand and relate to. When students exhibit these types of behaviors, workaholic teachers become more and more controlling. They might find themselves taking the pencil from the student and actually doing the work themselves so that something gets accomplished. As they become more frustrated, they may admonish the students for not bothering to think more clearly. Workaholics have to be careful not to take on too many tasks, or they may find themselves not being able to do any of their jobs well.

The favored learning style of the Workaholic is through thoughts. Workaholic teachers encourage their students to give thoughtful attention to questions and answers. They can be heard saying to students, "Now think about that," "Take time to think before you answer," or "What do you think about that?" Workaholic teachers give their students an abundance of information and data on the topics they teach and expect thorough, well-thought-out, and correctly done products from them.

A Workaholic teacher may:

1. Have a syllabus or schedule.

2. Be planned well in advance.

3. Come to work early and stay late.

4. Focus on work at the expense of the family.

5. Be a team leader or administrator.

6. Seek out and utilize new information.

7. Be up to date on administrative tasks.

8. Take on too much at the expense of quality.

9. Become impatient with those who do not produce.

10. Use "I think" as a frequent speech pattern.

Rebel Teachers

Rebel teachers are spontaneous, playful, creative, and fun. Their reactions to the world depend on their likes and dislikes and can change as their moods change. They like to have fun. They are creative, tend to be musical or artistic, and function best in an active environment that stimulates their creativity. Therefore, they frequently use methods such as drama, music, or group brainstorming to teach their classes. They tend to be kinesthetic learners themselves, so they frequently have their students actively participate in games, competitions, or other activities that get the students up and moving around. They find creative ways to illustrate the teaching points they want to stress and encourage their students to use their creativity. Frequently, they confound the administration because their rooms sometimes seem like bedlam. This works fine with Rebels and some Promoter students but frequently results in Workaholic and Persister students complaining that they cannot concentrate in that teacher's class. This type of teaching may invite extreme distress for Dreamer students who need quiet time and structure in order to learn.

A Rebel teacher may:

1. Use cartoons in their lessons.

2. Play music during class.

3. Have students act out roles in plays or stories.

4. Decorate the room with colorful posters.

5. Encourage creativity in their students.

6. Provide opportunities for their students to have fun in their class.

7. Set up games and competitions to encourage student participation.

8. Not meet deadlines for required reporting or administrative paperwork.

9. Use novel methods to teach lessons.

10. Establish a casual atmosphere in the classroom.

11. Not give enough information when assigning homework or class assignments.

12. Have active, noisy classrooms.

Promoter Teachers

Promoter teachers are resourceful, adaptable, and charming. They like action, excitement, and quick reward for anything they do. Consequently, not many Promoters become teachers. If they do teach, they usually teach physical education, industrial arts, or other active, hands-on subjects. They also enjoy coaching sports teams. They may teach for a few years and then move into a school administrative position that they consider more exciting and puts them center stage. Because Promoters are kinesthetic learners and need to move around, they include a lot of activity in their teaching methods. Promoters tend to be very direct in communicating. As a result, many of their students may incorrectly feel that their Promoter teachers are criticizing them harshly.

A Promoter teacher may:

1. Speak in a directive manner with the students.

2. Include many activities to get the students up and moving.

3. Teach the students how they can use the content of the lesson in real life.

4. Include competitive activities in class.

5. Hang action photos or pictures of heroes in the classroom.

6. Make deals with students.

7. Break lessons into small parts with rewards after each part is learned.

8. Teach the big picture before teaching the logical progressive steps leading to it.

9. Ignore required reports or administrative paperwork.

10. Attempt to manipulate students or fellow teachers.

Dreamer Teachers

Dreamer teachers usually have some of the other parts of their personality well developed, or they don't survive long in the school system with its competition for test scores, myriad paperwork, and accountability for student progress and behavior. However, Dreamer teachers bring a calmness, imagination, and reflectiveness to the classroom. They encourage students to probe deeply and think outside the box. They may display their daily schedule as a poem or a story in which the students become a part. They often teach through stories and metaphors drawing unique relationships between ideas and thoughts. They allow plenty of time for independent study and exploration of individual ideas and imaginative endeavors that tie arts, literature, history, music, science, and computers together in novel ways. They can often be found having deep discussions with individual students about topics they are exploring.

Dreamer teachers may do things in unique and unpredictable ways. Sometimes the novelty of their ideas keeps the interest of students who cause problems in other classrooms. However, Dreamer teachers are not good at direct confrontation. When students challenge them or argue with each other, Dreamer teachers use distraction or mediation techniques well to help resolve the problem. However, if the hostility becomes chronic, they may become very uncomfortable and withdraw from using any disciplinary measure.

Usually Dreamer teachers eat their lunch alone and use planning periods to regroup and process their thoughts about the events of the day. Although they do not contribute frequently in staff meetings, when they do share their suggestions, the ideas are often deep and complicated enough to require quite a bit of explanation. In the heat of a long agenda, it may be that few people take the time to think about their contributions, so their participation is often ignored or rejected by other teachers.

Teachers who are Dreamers may find themselves having difficulty keeping up with grading their students' assignments as well as the administrative paperwork required by the school system unless they have a strong Workaholic or Persister component to their personality. Many Dreamer teachers lose their inspiration for teaching, and it becomes too regimented for them to remain in the profession.

A Dreamer teacher may:

1. Relate seemingly unrelated ideas.

2. Provide opportunities for independent work.

3. Use original ways of teaching.

4. Encourage reflection.

5. Use interdisciplinary curriculum.

6. Give essay tests rather than tests that have only one right answer.

7. Create a safe environment for sharing unorthodox ideas.

8. Engage students in deep discussion of ideas.

9. Have little interest in the appearance of the classroom.

10. Find it difficult to keep current with administrative paperwork.

11. Shut down when there is excessive noise and conflict.

People are not made up of just one personality type. Each person has varying degrees of each type with their base being the strongest. Heather's personality profile (see figure 1.1) is the strongest in Persister, which is her base. Heather's strong Persister and Reactor parts make her a valued member of the staff. She takes a leadership role in the canned food and clothing drives for the less fortunate families of the school, reflecting her Persister and Reactor strengths. They are also evident in the look of her classroom, which has decorative and motivational posters such as "Think about Others," "Teamwork Is the Key" and "Always Do Your Best." Heather is a base Persister in a Reactor phase.

PHASE

A phase is the part of an individual's personality that determines a person's current motivation. It can be the base part of their personality structure, or they can change or "phase" so that their current motivation is determined by a different part of their personality. When a person experiences a phase change, the next-strongest part of his or her personality determines his or her motivation. These phase changes always follow in sequence the order of their personality structure; that is, if a person has a Persister base and Reactor is the next strongest, his or her first phase change will be to his or her Reactor part. If an individual experiences a second phase change, it will be determined by the next-strongest part of his or her personality. For example, if Heather were to experience a second phase change, her motivation would be determined by the Workaholic part of her personality. According to Kahler (1996), a phase lasts anywhere from several months to a lifetime. In North America, one-third of the population never experiences a phase change. On the other hand, some people have several phase changes in their lifetimes.

What causes a phase change? A phase change is a significant life change usually caused by periods of prolonged and severe distress. As people go through life, they experience stress in various areas of their lives. Sometimes this stress goes on for a long time and seems relentless, or sometimes many stressful events will occur at one time. If the person experiencing this distress deals with the underlying cause immediately, he or she may never experience a phase change. However, if the natural emotional response to the issue is postponed and internalized for a prolonged period of time, a phase change may ultimately occur when the person finally deals with this underlying emotion. At that time, interests in life, motivation, and the way in which the world is perceived may all change. When that happens, those who have gone through a phase change can often be observed taking up activities in which they previously had little interest. They may change careers, their behaviors may change, and the way they talk and dress may change. They may develop different friends, and frictions may develop in their current relationships. When people experience a phase change, their motivation changes, and they develop the traits in the next-strongest part of their personality structure. However, their base personality never changes and continues to be the part where they function most comfortably.

In Heather's case, she is a Persister in a Reactor phase. The traits of her Persister base—conscientious, dedicated, and observant—will always be her strongest characteristics. At some time in her life, however, she experienced a period of prolonged severe distress when life presented her with the issue unique to testing whether a Persister would phase. (It is not within the scope of this book to identify each issue and the dynamics involved in phasing—

only that phasing does occur and that a person's phase determines his or her motivational needs as well as predictable distress patterns.) When Heather worked through that period, she began developing the traits of her next-strongest personality part: Reactor. As a Persister in a Persister phase, she needed to hear that she was a good teacher, and she wanted to be respected. Although she still likes to hear that her opinions are taken seriously and her work is valued, now, in a Reactor phase, she is more interested in nurturing her students, and it has become important that they like her.

Heather is a Persister in a Reactor phase with a strong Workaholic component, but her other parts are not as well developed. The students who are the most likely to present problems for Heather are Rebels, Promoters, and Dreamers. As we look at student personality profiles in chapter 2, it is evident that the students Heather has the most difficulty relating to are the strongest in the very areas where Heather is the weakest.

The Students Arrive

Key 2: Know Your Students

Heather believes she has set up a classroom atmosphere where the students will do their best work as well as demonstrate respect for her and for each other. As the students arrive, Heather is outside her classroom with her roster greeting each student with a smile and directing each to his or her assigned seat. While Heather takes attendance, the students' first assignment is to copy the classroom rules and put them in their notebooks. Their homework will be to go over these rules with their parents, who will then sign off on them. The schedule for the day is already on the chalkboard:

Schedule for the Day

Opening—Pledge, copy rules
Getting to know you—Team-building activity
Reading—Reading assessment
Math—Review fractions
Visit computer lab—Standards for participation
Writing—Write a five-paragraph exposition on the most interesting thing you
  did over the summer.
Lunch/outside break
Literature—Listen to and discuss a story
Science—Check out textbook
Prepare to go home

As she surveys her class on their first day, the first thing Heather notices is that JP still has on his hat and sunglasses and is already out of his seat talking to Randi. He seems much more interested in showing her his new cell phone and portraying himself as "Mr. Cool" than completing the rule-writing assignment. Heather gently tells JP to return to his seat until he finishes copying the rules, and she conveys the same message to Randi. JP goes back to his seat, giving several of his buddies a high five as he passes their desks. He busily shuffles some papers to make it look like he is getting ready to do the assignment. However, as soon as Heather turns to help another student, JP is out of his seat at the pencil sharpener, where two of his friends just happen to be also. As she gives him "the look" (a technique she learned in her summer course), he waves and smiles and exclaims, "Just a minute, Ms. Thompson. I have to finish telling them something important!" A loud laugh comes from the group. Heather knows that they aren't taking her seriously. She again thinks back to her summer workshop on behavior management. She tries proximity control—moving closer to the group. JP looks up at her with his winning smile and says in his most charming voice, "OK, Ms. Thompson, we're going!" As he and his friends saunter back to their seats, she thinks, "This is my classroom, I'm the boss, and the sooner they learn this, the better!" So she states in a loud voice, "JP, I want these rules copied by 10:00 A.M., or you'll stay after school and do it!" The following conversation ensues:

JP: Give us a break. What's with writing down these dumb rules anyway! We got the picture from second grade.

HT: If you already know the rules, then I should see some evidence of it, which I don't!

JP: Whoa, Ms. Thompson, don't get all bent out of shape. Just got a little sidetracked here with my bros. Hey, got a deal for you. You catch someone breaking rules and make him write them down in his book. Don't punish us all before we even break your rules.

HT: But if we do that, your parents won't see the rules and sign off on them, and I require that for my class.

JP: I'll tell my mom the rules. Take my word for it. (grins, class laughs)

HT: For the last time, JP, I want you to sit down and copy these rules, or you'll be staying after school!

JP: Waste of my time. Not doing it! Not staying after school either!

Heather realized that she had just wasted a good deal of the class period arguing with JP in front of the class. Clearly, the other students would not see her as the authority unless she could get JP under control. She doubted if she could get JP to stay after school and would have to call his parents. She really needed to review the notes from her summer workshop on behavior management and see which strategies she could use with him. He was really a charming kid, and she wanted to have a positive relationship with him.

JP

PROMOTER STUDENTS

JP's personality is the strongest in Promoter. JP can be a positive, charming student who adapts to a variety of situations. However, he thrives on action and excitement and doesn't get a whole lot of either in school. Therefore, he creates his own dramas where he can be the star, often at the expense of others, including his teachers. He has a special knack for cornering his teachers and inciting arguments.

Promoters need to move around a lot and enjoy being center stage. They are persuasive and make great leaders, but because of their need for excitement, they often lead their peers into off-task and sometimes even dangerous activities that provide short-term excitement. Sometimes Promoters get labeled as attention-deficit/hyperactivity disorder (ADHD) because of their inability to sit still for long periods of time.

Promoters are kinesthetic learners and learn best when they are actively involved in a project (Pauley, Bradley, & Pauley 2002). They thrive on immediate rewards, so they must be able to see the practicality of an assignment and how an activity will benefit them, or they will not bother to do it. They do not respond well to regimentation, rigid rules, or repetitive tasks. If a class is not exciting enough for them, they will create their own thrills. They might set up two students to get into an argument with each other and then step back and watch, or they may cause a scene by blatantly arguing with a teacher or even throwing furniture. They usually come out the winner in a power struggle such as the one JP had with Ms. Thompson.

Promoters can surprise their teachers by how well they do in school when they are properly motivated. They often have the capacity to excel in sports, drama, and academics. They usually have lots of friends who are taken with their charm and adaptability. They set trends, dressing in the most up-to-date fashions and using the latest slang. You may see them in leadership positions, from student council president to gang leader. They enjoy competition and like to be top dog. Promoters like to look good and succeed, especially in front of other people, so they may blame others if they fail or someone attempts to make them look bad. For example, if they get a poor grade, they blame the teacher.

Promoter energy is not a strength for Heather, so it is more difficult for her to relate to her students who are Promoters. However, Heather can use her Persister and Workaholic parts to learn about what motivates a Promoter and apply those techniques on a systematic basis with her Promoter students. By doing this, she can also satisfy her Reactor part that wants to help each student get what he or she needs. It is also essential that Heather get her own needs met: recognition for being an important member of the staff and surrounding herself with a comforting environment both at home and at work will satisfy her strong Reactor part. Being praised and recognized for her achievements and her strong beliefs in the value of education will support and meet her Persister needs.

REBEL STUDENTS

While all this was going on, Randi (a Rebel student) was getting impatient. She started tapping her fingers on her desk and began talking to the girl next to her. Next she dropped her purse, and all her makeup fell on the floor. Finally, just as Heather was getting JP settled down, Randi got out of her seat and began to walk to the back of the room. As she got to the end of the aisle, she tripped and fell, yelling "Oops!" in a loud voice that caused the rest of the class to laugh. Randi got up and shouted at Patrick, a boy in the last seat:

RANDI: Stop tripping me.

PATRICK: I didn't trip you. You tripped over your own big feet.

RANDI (smirking): You did so trip me.

An argument ensued. Heather rushed to Randi's side to use proximity as a tool to intervene in order to regain control of the class:

HEATHER: Randi, go back to your seat.

RANDI: I have to go to the bathroom.

HEATHER: You just went to the bathroom.

RANDI (grinning): Well I have to go again.

HEATHER: You can go after this class. For now go back to your seat. We'll have a bathroom break as soon as we finish our math class.

RANDI (shouting): Math! Yuk! I hate math. Besides, I don't see why I have to go back to my seat. JP isn't in his seat.

Randi returned to her seat muttering to herself in a voice just loud enough to be heard by those around her. Heather heard Randi say, "this dumb school,"

Randi

"this dumb class," and "this dumb teacher." Heather decided to use the strategy of planned ignoring and get on with teaching the class. At the same time, she concluded that she really had to review her notes from her summer course in classroom management, or this was going to be a very long year with Randi.

Randi's strongest personality type is Rebel. She is creative, spontaneous, and playful. She loves music and is very artistic. She likes to have fun, and she filters situations, people, interactions, and observations through her likes and dislikes. Sometimes this is seen in wide mood swings. Because Randi does not have much fun in most of her classes, she does not like most of them. In fact, she finds most of her classes boring. Randi has a lot of energy for which she must be able to find an outlet. If there is activity-based teaching that she can actively participate in and if she has an opportunity to use her creativity, she will like the class and will do well in it. If she begins to get disinterested in a class, she may begin to squirm in her seat, tap her fingers, or talk to her neighbors. If she gets really bored, she may tune out and daydream, make a sarcastic comment to the teacher, or do something to make the class laugh. In extreme cases when she becomes really frustrated, she may swear at the teacher, throw chairs, tip over desks, and hit or kick other children.

Randi is spontaneous, so she tends to say what is on her mind, usually without thinking of possible consequences. These behaviors frequently get her into trouble, and she may spend a lot of time staying after school, in detention, or in in-school suspension or may even get expelled. Typical Rebel behaviors such as impulsivity, attention getting, inattentiveness, and tuning out get many Rebels labeled ADHD or emotionally disturbed. Frequently, these behaviors are the result of miscommunication between Randi and her teachers.

But it need not be this way. Rebels are very creative, and many Rebels are extremely bright. They have a good sense of humor and usually have a wide circle of friends. Most of their classmates like them because they are fun. However, they do not respond well to regimentation and rigid rules, and they hate to be ordered around. They test the rules and like to see what they can get away with. This includes their choice in clothing. They tend to dress in individualistic ways. Like Promoters, Rebels are kinesthetic learners (Pauley et al., 2002). They need to be actively involved and to experience everything themselves. They do not learn vicariously. Their favorite subjects usually are art, music, drama, and creative writing; however, they may also be interested in gym class and sports because of the opportunity to move around, have fun, and be creative. These are the classes that enable Rebels to get through the school day. Many Rebels do not like math. However, according to Gilbert (personal communication, 1999), there is some evidence that if Rebels have a math teacher who uses creative ways to teach them in the early grades, math may become one of their favorite subjects. If not, they may hate math for the rest of their lives.

WORKAHOLIC STUDENTS

Meanwhile, Wesley (the Workaholic), who looked disgusted with Randi and JP's antics, said in a loud voice, "Can we get back to work? I'm never going to get this assignment finished before we go to the computer lab if I can't concentrate!" Heather was a little embarrassed that she had taken so much instructional time to deal with Randi and JP, but she knew she must establish the rules and follow through, or soon they would be running the class. Heather reassured Wesley that he was doing a great job on his essay and that she was looking forward to him reading it to the class.

Workaholic students are task oriented. When a job is assigned to them, their main goal is to accomplish it so that it can be checked off the list. They almost always have their work completed on time, and it is usually done to the best of their ability. They tend to be serious and responsible students who appreciate a job well done. Therefore, when assigned to group projects, Workaholics are often not satisfied with the way that all group members attend to the task.

Wesley

They often take the leadership role in the group, and if they become nervous about the quality of the project, they may take on everyone's jobs in order to make sure they are done properly. Workaholics often hold leadership roles in the school, such as an officer in the student government or a member of the honor society.

Workaholics like their possessions set up in an organized fashion. Their notebooks are neat and systematized with each assignment in the proper category. They like to have their supplies organized as well and make use of such materials as color-coded folders and backpacks that are divided into sections. Their desks and lockers are neat and orderly.

Workaholics make use of personal digital assistants, computers, cell phones, and other electronic devices that help them organize their world and gather information. They tend to be serious students who believe that they should work first and play later. Their play often tends to be surfing the Web for information, watching a documentary on television, reading a news-magazine, or playing a computer game that involves increasing levels of difficulty. Workaholics appreciate teachers who structure the time and communicate this structure to the students. They prefer schedules and syllabi that let them know exactly when projects should start and end so that they can organize their time accordingly. They respond well to routines because they are predictable and let the Workaholic know exactly what is expected. Hard work is the major activity of Workaholics, and they need to be praised for the work that they put into their assignments as well as for their finished products.

PERSISTER STUDENTS

As Heather began to return to the front of the class, Patrick, a Persister student, complained, "It's not fair that Randi should get away with telling a lie in order to get me in trouble. I didn't trip her. I believe she deliberately fell to get me in trouble. She should be made to stay after school until she learns to follow the rules." Heather had been noticing all day that Patrick was a stickler for the rules. He got right to work copying the classroom rules when the assignment was given. He did, however, have a discussion with Heather about rule 3 in front of the other students. He wondered why he should respect and be kind to people who did not show these traits toward him. Heather reassured Patrick that at some later point she would continue this discussion with the class and

Patrick

get their input and that she was very interested in what Patrick had to say about the topic. This seemed to satisfy Patrick for the moment.

Persister students are auditory learners who perceive the world through their opinions (Pauley et al., 2002). They have an opinion about everything and tend to give them often. They are conscientious and dedicated and tend to follow class rules. In general, teachers like them because they want to do well in school and usually do not cause problems. Because they view the world as a serious place, they do not appreciate classmates who fool around or ignore class rules. Frequently, they criticize those classmates and just as often get told to mind their own business. This usually does not bother them because they tend not to care if people like them. In fact, because they believe it is their duty to help people be all that they can be, they may view peer rejection as part of the price they pay for doing their duty. Consequently, they continue to point out when their classmates are not on task. For this reason and because they do not get close to people until they know they can trust them implicitly, Persister students usually do not have many friends—usually only one or two close friends in whom they can confide (Pauley et al., 2002).

Although Persister students rarely will win any popularity contest with their classmates, they frequently gravitate to leadership positions in projects they believe in because they are driven to succeed and have an ability to stick to a task until it is completed successfully. Teachers frequently recognize this and appoint them to be project leaders. If someone else is appointed leader and the project appears to be floundering, Persister students may step in and become the unofficial leader because of their determination to succeed at any project in which they believe.

REACTOR STUDENTS

As Heather made her way to the front of the room, Raydia (a Reactor) spilled her bottle of water all over the papers on her desk. She began to cry and berate herself. "I am so stupid," she muttered. Heather went to stand beside Raydia and assured her that she was not stupid. She told Raydia to clean up the mess and get back to work and not to worry about it. Raydia looked dubious but, still sniffling, followed her teacher's directions. She continued to look sad until Heather asked her to be a buddy for a new girl in class, and then Raydia beamed with delight.

Reactor students are visual learners who are compassionate, sensitive, and warm (Pauley et al., 2002). They perceive the world through their emotions. They feel first, and they want people to feel with them. They have excellent interpersonal skills and form close relationships with other classmates very quickly. They are good at nurturing others and feel good when others show caring for them in return. They like people and do their best work when surrounded by others who like them. Because of their strong desire for approval, they frequently put off getting their own needs met and spend a lot of their energy figuring out how to please others. They want everyone to feel comfortable, and they feel very ill at ease when people argue or fight around them. They are good at creating harmony and at welcoming newcomers into a group. Reactors do well as peer tutors, peer advocates, or peer mediators because they instinctively work for win-win solutions to problems.

Raydia

DREAMER STUDENTS

As the students continued to work on their writing assignment "The Most Interesting Thing I Did on My Summer Vacation," Heather noticed that Daisy, who had subtly moved her seat away from the other students, was looking out the window with a blank look on her face. "Daisy, are you all right?" Heather asked. Daisy nodded, and Heather continued surveying the room. When she glanced at Daisy again, she still had a blank look on her face, so Heather walked over and stood next to her desk. She noticed that Daisy's paper was blank. "Daisy, you have to start the assignment," Heather told her in a firm voice. Daisy slowly reached for the paper and began to write. When it was time to go to lunch, Heather announced that the students would read their papers to the class when they returned, and then she dismissed the class.

After everyone left, she noticed that Daisy was still at her desk writing. Again, she walked over and stood next to the desk and saw that Daisy was still working on her paper. "Daisy, it's time to go to lunch now." "I want to finish this," replied Daisy. "I'm sorry, Daisy, but you have only yourself to blame. If you had started writing when you were supposed to, you would be done by now. You'll just have to live with what you have. Go to lunch now." Daisy went out the door looking dejected. Curious, Heather picked up Daisy's paper and read it. Her family had gone camping in the mountains, and every morning Daisy's job was to walk on the trail from their campsite to the campground store and bring back a quart of milk for breakfast. Walking on the trail by herself, Daisy had noticed the early morning light, the birds, and once a deer bounding away from her. On her paper she was carefully and artfully describing these events, choosing exactly the right words. Heather was amazed. During Daisy's blank looks, was she reliving the walks and organizing what she wanted to say? Heather wondered how she could accommodate this child in a busy classroom where things had to be done on time. She felt frustrated that such a bright student sat in her classroom and that her imaginative ideas were not likely to be reflected on the standardized assessments required by the school district.

Daisy's strongest personality type is Dreamer. Dreamer students are reflective and calm and the most imaginative of all the personality types. They need some alone time and shut down when they get overwhelmed. It takes them some time to engage in a project, and once engaged, they are reluctant to let go until they are finished. For this reason, they are often misdiagnosed as attention deficit disorder (without hyperactivity). When asked to read work or explain ideas in class, they often need more time and attention on the part of the teacher and their classmates to truly share their insights, which can be complex and involve seemingly unrelated topics. Many people who decide to become teachers don't have much Dreamer energy, so they are unaware of the processing and thought time that Dreamers need to comprehend and think through the concepts presented in class and to formulate responses to them. Because most teachers prefer to interact with other people, many may not realize that Dreamer students need their own space and some alone time in order to be more prepared to pay attention in class. Even when teachers know what motivates Dreamers, it is hard to provide this type of attention and space within the school realm.

Because of their well-developed imaginations, Dreamers see connections to ideas and concepts that the other types do not see. For this reason, they may have problems on multiple-choice tests because they see so many possibilities that to them there may not be only one right answer. They are so low key that they frequently get overlooked in the classroom, and because they are so quiet, people sometimes get the impression that they are not very intelligent or are not paying attention. In truth, many Dreamers are very intelligent. For example, Einstein, Michelangelo, and Thoreau were all Dreamers.

Dreamer students are very introspective. Because of their insights into themselves and others, they frequently make good writers. When they are encouraged to use their imaginations in class, they can be very successful. However, their teachers have to be understanding enough to accept work that may be quite unique and may differ somewhat from the intent of the assign-

Daisy

ment or from the work of the other students. In addition, Dreamers have difficulty prioritizing more than one or two tasks at a time. Therefore, teachers
may need to enlist the aid of another student or parent to help their Dreamer
students stay on task. They need help deciding the order in which they will do
multiple tasks, such as their homework assignments. In addition, Dreamer
students need some alone time every day. Unfortunately, they seldom are able
to be alone in school, so they frequently feel that they are being suffocated.
They also have a problem dealing with noise and confusion. They become
overwhelmed. When that happens, they shut down.

Dreamer students frequently are loners. They are not influenced by current
fashion or by the latest fads. They usually dress for comfort and wear clothes
that are appropriate for the weather. Many Dreamers are not socially adept
and do not have many friends in school. They realize they are different from
the other students, and because they make up a small percentage of the population, they may not meet other students who are like them. As a result,
Dreamer students may come to think of themselves as weird or dumb. Because
Dreamer students are different from their classmates, other students may
make fun of them, call them derogatory names, or bully them. Unless teachers
are careful, they may inadvertently contribute to the negative self-image that
Dreamer students might have of themselves.

Heather could see that her work for the school year was clearly cut out for
her. She was confident that many of her students, including Raydia, Patrick,
and Wesley, would thrive in her classroom and reflect well on the school. However, she was worried about how she would accommodate JP, Daisy, and
Randi.

3

Traditional Behavior Management Methods

Key 3: Examine Current Strategies

As a seasoned teacher, Heather has read many books and has attended a variety of workshops on classroom and behavior management. While she has found numerous preventive and interventive strategies that have worked with many of her students and she has had a hand in helping turn around students who were heading in the wrong direction, there is still a handful every year that she can't seem to reach.

Before the school year began, Heather had enthusiastically enrolled in a summer classroom management course with other teachers where they explored various educational philosophies and child development theories geared to helping teachers become better classroom managers. In this chapter, we will examine some of these more widely known and used management philosophies and strategies. We will also see what happens when Heather eventually learns about the Process Communication Model® (PCM), how she examines the effectiveness of these various strategies with different personality types, and how she sharpens her skills for reaching all her students.

Classroom management techniques have come a long way over the years. Old stereotypes of behavior management or "classroom control," such as making students sit in the corner with a dunce cap, requiring them to write "I will not talk in class" one hundred times, or administering a sound rap on the knuckles, have been replaced with more modern versions of humiliation and exclusion, such as sending students to the principal or to detention, yelling at students, sarcastic put-downs, and singling out misbehaving students so that they are ultimately rejected by peers and teachers alike. Most classroom management issues have control as the ultimate goal—students who want control of their school lives vying for power with teachers who believe they need to be the ultimate authority in their classrooms.

It would be ideal if all students could manage their own behavior so that teachers could instruct in their most effective fashion. In fact, often students are expected to come to school able to manage their own behavior in a way that makes them available for learning. However, anyone who has been in charge of a classroom knows this is not always the case. When teachers are first confronted with students who they consider unruly, impolite, aggressive, or indifferent, they usually have an emotional reaction and may respond accordingly by yelling, threatening, punishing, isolating, or getting into a public power struggle. Is this high-stress, fearful environment really creating classrooms that are conducive to learning? Rather than the curriculum being the focus, the center of attention for both the teacher and the other students becomes the misbehaving student. These ineffective techniques leave the teacher exhausted and the students turned off by school. Heather's motivation for taking the summer workshop in behavior management was to engage in fewer of these behaviors and learn strategies that would enable her to use her instructional time most effectively. The following is some of what she learned.

THE NEED FOR EFFECTIVE MANAGEMENT IN THE CLASSROOM

Heather knew that classroom disruption and behavior problems significantly interfere with teaching and learning (Cotton, 1990). However, she was surprised to find out just how prevalent this phenomenon was. Cotton (1990) states that up to 50 percent of instructional time is used to deal with behavior issues rather than academic content. Levin and Nolan (1991) found evidence that between 30 and 80 percent of classroom time is lost to disciplinary issues. If teachers can reduce the amount of time that they spend on behavior problems, it follows that they will increase the amount of time spent teaching content and that academic achievement will improve. Today's teachers are struggling to ensure that every child makes adequate yearly progress in order to conform to the No Child Left Behind Act. Teachers are judged to be effective when their students significantly increase their academic achievement.

However, as Marzano (2003a) points out, "Effective teaching and learning cannot take place in a poorly managed classroom" (p. 1). Fortunately, research supports the premise that classroom management techniques can be learned and that teachers can become more successful as they gather and use effective management strategies (Borg & Ascione, 1982).

SETTING UP THE CLASSROOM

One of the first things a teacher can do to manage the classroom is to set up a positive, proactive learning environment. Marzano (2003b) identifies several research-based strategies that have helped teachers be successful, the first of which is to set up classroom rules and procedures so that they are clear to everyone. This is best done in the form of a discussion with plenty of student input not only into classroom rules but also into the rewards and consequences. Students are much more likely to adhere to a set of rules that they helped establish than those they perceive are forced on them (Curwin & Mendler, 1988; Evertson et al., 1997; Kohn, 1996; Stronge, 2002). It is important to explain the classroom standards clearly and state the reasons for them. Posting them so that they are highly visible to both the teacher and students so they can frequently be referred to can help reinforce consistency in the classroom. It is well worth the "front-load" time to clearly establish these standards with buy-in from the students so that ultimately more time can be devoted to teaching and learning.

PROCEDURES AND ROUTINES

The second factor to consider for sound classroom management is establishing classroom procedures and routines. Is there a warm-up on the board every day that has to be done by a certain time? Where does homework go? Do you greet your students at the door each morning? Do we say the pledge to the flag each day? Students with behavioral and emotional issues often have difficulty when routines are disrupted. If what happens every day is different, students who have to test the limits will be testing them every day. Fewer behavior problems occur in classrooms that adhere to established routines (Carpenter, Musy, & King-Sears, 1997; Englert, 1984).

Students need to be able to easily access the learning materials they will need, such as books, papers, manipulatives, and equipment (e.g., the pencil sharpener), with a minimum of disruption to instruction. Placement of these materials is crucial for maximum efficiency and support of instructional activities. Desk arrangement and seating of students should be done so that the teacher is able to monitor students at all times, even when meeting with individuals or small groups.

SURFACE MANAGEMENT TECHNIQUES

A third issue is the use of surface management to maintain a classroom where learning is the primary activity. Surface management consists of those techniques that teachers use unobtrusively to address student behavior that is off task while maintaining fluid instruction. This type of management also addresses potential misbehavior before it becomes a major problem. Marzano (2003a) suggests a hierarchy of methods, including the following:

- Proximity (standing near a student who may be about to get into trouble)
- Signal interference (using a signal such as lights out, clapping patterns, or a rain stick to get students' attention)
- Verbal reminders
- A firm, direct command to cease the inappropriate behavior

Carpenter et al. (1997) have listed teacher behaviors from least to most intrusive that can support desired student behaviors. These include some of the same techniques as Marzano, such as signal interference and proximity. They also suggest the following:

- Planned ignoring
- Interest boosting—interjecting a novel activity or way of presenting the material
- Tension decontamination—using humor to reduce anxiety
- Restructuring the lesson
- Removing seductive objects
- Antiseptic bounce—temporarily removing students from a situation by sending them to another classroom with a note or asking them to run an errand
- Private reprimands

- Modeling and recognizing appropriate behaviors (e.g., I want to thank those of you who got ready so quickly)

Most students respond positively to encouraging feedback. Whether this is done publicly can depend on the age, experience, and personality of the student. In fact, there are many ways to catch students "being good" and give them positive feedback, whether it be through recognizing their behavior, their humor, their artwork, their academic products, or their perceptiveness.

Although these teacher behaviors are deliberate and require thought rather than reaction, they can be done quickly and privately with minimal disruption to the instructional program and without getting into a power struggle. Many teachers have learned to use a signal or proximity without a break in their teaching. This limits disruptions for the other students while letting those who are off task know that they should not continue with their behavior.

In addition to learning about these techniques, the teachers participating in the summer workshop examined several websites that address classroom management issues.

These included the following:

- http://www.honorlevel.com/techniques.xml
- http://www.ldonline.org/ld_indepth/teaching_techniques/class_manage .html
- http://educ.indiana.edu/cas/tt/v1i2/what.html
- www.interventioncentral.org
- www.masterteacher.com
- www.disciplinehelp.com
- www.schoolbehavior.com
- www.behavioradvisor.com
- www.projectiveachieve.info
- www.nea.org/helpfrom/growing/works4me/manage/index.html

CLASSROOM MANAGEMENT STYLES AND MODELS

Those students who have had very little success in the school setting are not always responsive to surface management techniques. Sometimes these students need more external motivation. Heather's summer workshop examined a number of models of classroom management techniques that included the following:

1. Assertive Discipline (Canter, 1989) is based on the premise that children respond positively to classroom environments where the teacher is in charge, the rules are clear, and the students know that the teacher will control student behavior. According to the underlying philosophy of this model, students understand the need for punishment for inappropriate behavior. Teachers are confident of their position. They know they are in charge in their dealings with students and are persistent and firm as well as consistent in verbal and nonverbal communication. "Assertive teachers establish limits for their students and enforce them" (Edwards, 1993, p. 61).

2. Reality Therapy (Glasser, 1990) is based on the belief that students really want to control their own environment and that punishment will only cause students to rebel against such firm teacher control. This theory is based on human needs for social relationships that include love, control, freedom, and fun. The teacher's role should focus on helping students find ways to behave appropriately that meet these needs. Students must own their misbehavior, and the teacher's role is to guide them to figure out a different plan for dealing with situations that caused them to misbehave.

3. The Kounin Model (Kounin, 1970) emphasizes teacher "withitness"—having eyes in the back of your head and maintaining control by being aware of what is going on in the classroom with all students at all times. The theory is that students will behave better when teachers are clear about the misbehavior, provide direction in what is an appropriate replacement behavior, and give them credible reasons for their request for the "desist" of certain behaviors.

4. Logical Consequences (Dreikurs, Grunwald, & Pepper, 1982) is based on understanding the goals of misbehavior and then developing consequences with the students so that they are the most logical and natural and the students know what to expect. This model has as its premise that everyone needs to belong and to be accepted. Teachers examine the motivators of power, attention, revenge, and inadequacy and then redirect students to replacement goals by employing consequences that have a logical connection to the misbehavior.

5. Operant Conditioning or Behavior Modification is based on the work of B. F. Skinner and others (Edwards, 1993; Lefrancois, 1988). The operant conditioning theory has evolved into "contingencies," "shaping," "differential reinforcement," and other token economy systems that offer students rewards and/or consequences for engaging in specific behaviors. The goal is to extinguish inappropriate behaviors, usually by enforcing desired ones. Often this is done through the development of a behavioral contract for a specific student with explicit rewards and/or consequences built in for reinforcers. One crucial factor to remember when implementing this type of behavioral system is to involve the student in the development of the target behaviors and in the decision about rewards and punishments. When students have input into these types of systems, they are likely to work better. When these "contracts" are developed solely by the educators, they are really not contracts at all. Rather, they tend to be rules that have been made up by adults with rewards and consequences they believe are valuable to the student. Without student input, these interventions are rarely successful.

6. Discipline with Dignity (Curwin & Mendler, 1988) suggests a three-pronged approach of prevention, action, and resolution based on mutual respect and dignity. Consequences based on a social contract are used only when students are completely out of control. This "discipline program" puts the onus for behavior management on the teacher through the implementation of sound teaching performance.

Other theorists have criticized management programs that contain any punishments or consequences for students. Brendtro, Brokenleg, and van Bockern (1998) present us with a Native American view of responding to "troubled children" that encompasses instilling in them the traits of responsibility, respect, caring, and knowledge rather than using punitive measures. Alfie Kohn (1996) sharply criticizes both punishment and rewards as merely meanness or bribes that instill fear and do nothing to help children control their own behavior. However, the research does not support the complete elimination of rewards and consequences as sound management techniques (Stage & Quiroz, 1997).

Caution must be exercised before adopting any one model as a classroom-, school- or system-wide method that will quell all behavior problems. Many school systems have fallen into the trap of forcing all students into a "one-size fits all" management system they believe should work for everyone. However, just as teachers know that instruction often must be individualized, they have also found that management techniques have to be tailored to the individual. Brophy and Evertson (1976) as well as Wubbels, Brekelmans, van Tartwijk, and Admiral (1999) found that teachers who took personal responsibility for their classrooms, had a sense of inner control, and solicited student input and cooperation were perceived as the most positive by students and had classrooms that made the most academic progress. Without a system that employs multiple techniques, there still will be students whom teachers consistently have trouble reaching. Frequently, these students are those who have vastly different personality structures from their teachers and from other authority figures who are setting the behavioral standards.

ADDING PROCESS COMMUNICATION TO THE MIX

As the school year progressed, Heather realized that several of the techniques from her summer workshop that she was implementing were having a positive effect on many of her students. However, she was still in a quandary about the best ways to approach Randi, JP, and Daisy. Sometimes her interventions were successful, and sometimes they were not. None of these students was performing academically as well as Heather had hoped.

That fall, Heather's school offered a course on Process Communication. She learned about the six personality types, their needs, and the mismatches that often occur between students and teachers of different types. In thinking over what she had learned in both workshops, Heather realized that the various personality types in her classroom were responding differently to the techniques she was using.

MEETING THE NEEDS OF EACH PERSONALITY TYPE

As Heather reviewed her notes and thought further about what she had learned in the summer behavior management course, she began to be able to pick and choose from each of the theoretical models on the basis of the new knowledge she was learning in her Process Communication class. The "withitness" that Kounin (1970) emphasized was an important factor in taking the barometer of her classroom and knowing when to change the activity, vary her voice tone, or incorporate physical movement in order to help students get their needs met before their behavior got out of hand. She decided to incorporate advice from Brophy (1996), who found that those teachers who had the best-managed classrooms used different interventions, depending on the various types of students found in today's classrooms. This theory supported what she was learning in the PCM course—that she could manage her classroom better if she made the decision about how to approach each student personally and how to present academic material so that it appealed to each of the personality types (Pauley, Bradley, & Pauley, 2002).

She realized that the theories of Curwin and Mendler, Brendtro et al., and Kohn could work for any student. Based on helping students get their needs met positively, these theories could be further honed by examining the needs of each personality type and selecting teacher behaviors that would meet these needs. Pauley et al. (2002) delineate the needs of each of the types of students. They point out that Promoters like JP need to be active and respond to being involved in something they consider exciting during the school day. Rebels like Randi need to have fun in order to energize the parts of their personality needed for classroom work. Dreamers need some time without outside stimulation so that they can process and make meaning from material that has been presented. They also benefit by structure and prioritizing. A warm and emotionally safe atmosphere and being appreciated for who they are help to meet the needs of Reactors like Raydia. Wesley, the Workaholic, needs to be recognized for his academic accomplishments and also needs to know the schedule and when things are due. Finally, Patrick and other Persisters need opportunities to share their opinions and have them validated. They also need to be recognized for their high-quality work and good ideas. The needs of each personality type are discussed in more detail in chapter 4.

As Heather learned more about the personality types of her students, she incorporated the information and techniques she already knew and made better decisions about which strategies to use with each student. For instance, she realized that signal interference or using some type of gesture to signify a student is off task worked well with Rebels and Promoters, especially when it was a secret signal that was developed just between them. It could even be slightly humorous, such as head scratching or a series of hand gestures known only to the student and teacher. Interest boosting worked with all the types, and she vowed to use this often. Tension decontamination or using humor worked well with Rebels and Promoters because it broke up any tension that was building.

It also helped maintain the attention of the other types. Telling a student to cease his or her inappropriate behavior worked best with Dreamers and Promoters who responded best when told what to do but was a disaster with Rebels who frequently argued with the mandate or got into a power struggle with her. Antiseptic bounce—removing students by sending them on errands—was an effective intervention for Promoters or Rebels who need to move around and for Dreamers who need some alone time.

Of the classroom discipline models, Heather found that Assertive Discipline appealed to Workaholic and Persister students who responded well to firm, known rules and to Reactors who need to know that someone is in charge and will make the classroom a safe place. Rebels, however, respond poorly to rigid rules and may want to argue or purposefully get off task to see what reaction they can evoke. Reality therapy, which is based on student analysis of the problem, appealed most to Workaholics who specialize in data gathering and analysis and to Reactors because it gave them an opportunity to talk through the situation in a nonthreatening atmosphere.

The Kounin Model and the Logical Consequences model are based on logic:

1. Pointing out the misbehavior
2. Letting students know why it is inappropriate
3. Giving them something else to do instead

Consequences are logical and relate to the misbehavior. This logical appeal works best with Workaholics and Persisters. Promoters, on the other hand, may use this approach as an opportunity to argue about who is right, and it might set up Rebels to act out.

Behavior Modification is criticized by behavioral specialists such as Kohn, Brendtro et al., and Curwin and Mendler as a program of coercion and bribery. These researchers believe that students who are part of these types of programs do not develop intrinsic motivation to behave. However, Evertson, Emmer, Clements, and Worsham (1997) highlight the usefulness of using a reward system on a limited basis and encourage it as an alternative to lowering academic expectations or using random threats and punishments. Those students with high Promoter energy who like quick rewards may respond positively to a contract. For the contract to succeed, however, it is essential that the students have input into the terms of the contract, that the reward is something they value and will work toward, and that the payoffs are frequent enough to be motivating to the Promoter.

Heather now knows that if she implements a variety of teaching and management techniques based on reaching each personality type, she can reduce the number of behavior problems in her class. Having learned the concepts of Process Communication, she can sharpen her skills by knowing how the various techniques will meet the needs of the personality types of her students and ensure that she is offering them what they require in order to be able to make the best academic progress.

Variety, Novelty, and Humor

With so much emphasis on student achievement and increasing test scores, what place do variety, novelty, and humor have in the classroom? We have already examined the importance of maintaining students' academic focus while at the same time meeting their basic human and psychological needs in order for them to be in a state conducive to learning. Variation of presentation style can go a long way in getting students' attention, which is often the first step in motivating them to get maximum benefit from instruction. Using the lyrics of popular music, providing hands-on science experiences, dressing up like a historical character, and dividing food into fractional parts are examples of ways to capture student attention and keep them focused on the lesson. Breaking lectures and discussions into small parts (no longer than 15 minutes) and interspersing them with opportunities for students to discuss and/or reflect on the ideas alone or with a partner helps them digest the material and become more involved in the learning process (Jensen, 1995; Levin & Nolan, 1991). When everyone wants to speak at once or she is greeted with blank stares, one teacher says to her students, "Talk at your tables" as a way to get them to share their ideas and process information.

Evertson et al. (1984) recommend including interesting and special items in the classroom as motivators and teaching tools. Aquariums, bulletin boards, plants, computers, and science or history tables provide students with areas of interest as well as visual and kinesthetic learning opportunities. Centers or learning zones provide an area to study about a special activity or topic, and comfortable and stimulating book corners encourage students to select and read books on their own.

In order to maximize "brain-based learning," Jensen (1995) suggests the following:

- Use videos, music, discussion, and group study sessions
- "Make the room rich with colorful poster, pictures, charts, mobiles and mind maps" (p. 10)
- Plan field trips, simulations, and real-life projects
- Let students express what they know through music, maps, role play, journals, models movement, and artwork
- Utilize learning zones, partner learning, and individualized mastery learning
- Provide choices as often as possible

It is difficult for teachers to maintain student attention, especially that of Rebels and Promoters, when the lesson starts off slowly. Jensen suggests attention getters to begin lessons such as the use of music, making eye contact with each student, playing an instrument, putting on a special hat, clapping patterns, and even doing a magic trick. Imagine the appeal and intrigue to Rebels and Promoters as well as the other personality types as they eagerly await what comes next!

Humor can be used by teachers in a variety of ways. As a surface management technique, it can be used to diffuse a potentially volatile situation and redirect students to appropriate behavior. For example, one teacher renames common objects (i.e., pencils become gloppers). When she asks a student who is off task, "Where is your glopper?" it usually gets a smile and produces on-task behavior without a confrontation. Telling a joke or showing a comic related to the lesson at the beginning of class can be used as an attention getter for all personality types and ensures that Rebels start the class getting their need met for having fun (Pauley et al., 2002).

STUDENT–TEACHER RELATIONSHIPS

"Without the foundation of a good relationship students commonly resist rules and procedures along with the consequent discipline actions" (Marzano, 2003a, p. 41). "Some learners are not receptive to learning until a relationship with the teacher has been established" (Jensen, 1995, p. 116). Research supports that problems of students and teachers relating negatively to each other exacerbates and can even cause behavior problems (Sheets & Gay, 1996).

Pauley et al. (2002) emphasize the importance of the relationship between students of all personality types and their teachers to overall student success in school. For example, Persisters need to respect and admire their teachers and know that the assignments they are being given are worthwhile. Otherwise, they have a hard time buying in to the value of what is going on in the classroom. They may spend their time finding fault with the teacher and the other students and become distracted from their schoolwork.

The relationship between Reactors and their teachers is paramount. Reactors must feel liked and valued by the teacher. If they feel that the teacher doesn't like them, they can become greatly distressed and may manifest memory problems, clumsiness, or poor self-esteem that affects the quality of their schoolwork.

The academic progress of Promoters is profoundly affected by the relationships they establish with their teachers. In their book *Here's How to Reach Me*, Pauley et al. (2002) give this example from a Promoter: "If I have a good relationship with a teacher, I can learn anything. If I don't have a good relationship, I have trouble learning anything" (p. 90). Many Promoters get off on the wrong foot with their teachers because of vast differences in their personality energy. It is important to know that taking the time and effort to establish positive relationships with Promoters can go a long way toward reducing behavior problems while enhancing their academic progress.

If Rebel students connect with their teachers and like their classes, their creativity will soar, and they will be motivated to do well on academic tasks. Often the report card of a Rebel is erratic, with grades ranging from A to F, depending on whether there is a positive or negative relationship developed between the student and teacher. If their talents are recognized and they perceive the teacher and/or the class as "fun," they are more motivated to complete their assignments and will make significant progress in their academic subjects.

Because Workaholics are self-driven to achieve in their academic tasks, they will usually do what it takes to succeed. However, their progress can be impeded if they think they cannot take a teacher seriously, if time frames are not adhered to, or if they mistrust the information that is given to them by the instructor.

The school culture is often in conflict with the style of Dreamers, and many wish they could avoid being in the classroom altogether. However, if a teacher shows acceptance of and respect for the uniqueness of the ideas and presenta-

tion style of Dreamer students, an alliance between Dreamers and their teachers can be formed. Dreamer students are more likely to value and participate
in school activities if their teachers convey to them that their way of thinking
is valued, let them know they will be provided with some private time and
space, and show them the importance of obtaining credibility through adher-
ing to basic classroom standards so that they can use and share their talents.

Good student–teacher relationships have a positive impact on student
achievement. Marzano (2003a) states, "Virtually anything you do to show
interest in students as individuals has a positive impact on their learning"
(p. 53). When teachers take the time and energy to identify the personality types
of their students and utilize specific ways of relating to them, positive relationships will likely develop. These relationships can result in students getting their
needs met during the school day, in less time being taken from instruction to
address behavior problems, and in increased academic achievement.

4

Motivating Students of All Types

Key 4: Motivate by Type

One of the most important things Heather was learning in the Process Communication course was that each of the personality types has specific motivators or incentives that are essential in order for them to thrive and perform in the classroom. (These motivators were examined briefly in chapter 3.) As Heather continued to learn about the incentives that appealed the most to each type of student, she thought back over the first few weeks of school. She remembered when she complemented Wesley, who was a Workaholic, on his essay. Even though he was upset that so much time was taken in the discussion with Randi and JP, he seemed to calm down when his work was given positive recognition and he was able to resume his work. In light of the new information she had learned in her Process Communication Model® (PCM) course, the success of that intervention made sense, as Workaholics need recognition for their work. When she reassured Patrick (a Persister) that she was interested in his opinion about the classroom rules and would give him a chance to share that with the class, he was able to resume his concentration on the task at hand. She realized she had validated his values and opinions. And she had stumbled on just the right solution to get Raydia to stop crying. When she assigned her to be a buddy for a new student, she met Raydia's need to be recognized for her warmth and her ability to reach out to others.

Certainly, a key to keeping her students on task and motivated was knowing about and finding ways to meet the needs of each of her students. Gilbert

describes these motivational needs as "those things that motivate us when we get them and distress us when we do not" (Gilbert, 2004, p. 47). Although Heather's teaching naturally consisted of ways to motivate students like Patrick, Raydia, and Wesley, some of the concepts she learned in her PCM course about meeting needs and essential motivators based on personality type were new to her, and she had never considered them before. For instance, because her energy was high in Persister, Reactor, and Workaholic, she never realized that some students worked better if they played first. She had always considered "play" a reward to be given after work was complete. Additionally, she knew from previous courses and workshops that multisensory teaching was important, but she was finding out just how important.

Heather's biggest challenges continued to be students like JP, Randi, and Daisy. She learned that Promoters like JP were motivated by action and that Randi needed to have fun. Daisy could use more structure and would benefit by time to work quietly and alone. All these students had talents that Heather wanted to find more ways to tap into. But how was she going to find the time, ideas, and resources to address the needs of these children so that she could nurture their skills and talents?

WHAT HAPPENS WHEN NEEDS ARE NOT MET, AND WHAT CAN BE DONE ABOUT IT?

The motivators and incentives identified for each personality type are absolutely necessary for each of them to experience several times during the school day so that students and their teachers can accomplish the various tasks that schools require. If these motivators or needs are not addressed in a positive way, then negative behaviors will ensue.

Personality Types and Motivators

Personality Type	Motivators
Reactor	Recognition of person and sensory
Workaholic	Recognition for work and time structure
Persister	Recognition for work and conviction
Dreamer	Solitude and direction
Rebel	Playful contact
Promoter	Incidence

MOTIVATING PROMOTERS

For example, Promoter students must have action and excitement, or what Kahler calls "incidence." School is often not exciting enough for Promoters, so they frequently make their own excitement and then find themselves in trouble. They become easily bored sitting in the classroom, and if activity and movement are not built into the school day, they will create opportunities to move around. When the classroom task requires that they stay in their seats and listen for long periods of time, they may get up and walk around at inappropriate times. They also create drama in the classroom by setting up pranks and conflicts, and sometimes they behave in ways they know will get them removed from class in order to get themselves out of the classroom atmosphere altogether. When their needs to be active and get their adrenaline pumping are not met during the school day, it is essential for them to get these needs met in other ways, and Promoters are quite inventive about generating other options. Providing Promoters with some movement, competition, and the occasional unexpected response, such as answering a question with a song or as a different character, helps keep things interesting and enticing to them.

What motivates students like JP who are Promoters? What types of things can Heather do to get JP to be more cooperative and to be more involved in his schoolwork? During the afternoon of the first day of school, Heather had selected JP to pass out the science books. She noticed he took this job seriously and right afterward was able to concentrate better. She also became aware that after he had a chance to move around, such as going to lunch or changing classes, he was the most attentive. However, if the task was sedentary and required a lot of writing, it was almost certain that he could be found wandering around the room. Therefore, if Heather knows that JP needs action and excitement, she can build in this type of individual support. Asking him to pass out supplies, letting him run the PowerPoint presentation, or putting him in charge of being the scorekeeper puts him in an involving leadership role while at the same time requiring and maintaining his attention to the task. Additionally, Promoters need to move around and get some physical activity in order to be able to sit and concentrate. Therefore, Heather will want to be sure to plan activities that contain movement, competition, game formats, and drama so that he has opportunities to be in motion, especially right before an activity that will take a great deal of sitting and/or concentration. Although these types of activities may be difficult and strange for her at first, as she becomes more comfortable with them, she will see positive results with JP and her other Promoter students.

Promoter students also need to see the immediate connection of what they are learning to their own lives. If Heather can ensure that she includes practical applications of the lessons she is teaching, then JP can see the relevance of the academic material to his current life. Providing short-term rewards, such as extra computer time for successful completion of an assignment, and using humor (not sarcasm) will go a long way with Promoters. Occasionally, making deals with them helps Promoters stay motivated and facilitates their desire to be important and have power. For example, one math teacher would assign ten problems for homework each night. Frequently, the Promoters would complain that ten problems were too many. The math teacher made a deal with the class. She would cut cards with one student, high card wins. If the student got the high card, the class need do only five problems on the condition that everyone in the class turned in the completed assignment and all the problems were correct. If not, the five they did not do that night would be added to their assignment the following night. The Promoter students jumped at the chance to be the one to cut the cards. The Promoter students made sure that everyone did their homework and enlisted the aid of the Workaholics and Persisters to make sure that everyone had all the problems done correctly. This is really win-win learning. The Promoter student wins because he or she gets to look good to his or her peers, the Workaholics and Persisters win because they receive recognition for their academic ability, the class wins because they learn the skills and concepts, and the teacher wins because everyone in the class has done the assignment and learned the subject matter. When Promoters experience learning as active and exciting, they are less likely to engage in behaviors that are negative and distracting.

MOTIVATING REBELS

Having fun is what motivates a Rebel. If Rebels can have some fun or "playful contact" before they are required to work, it is easier for them to access those parts of their personalities that are not so strong (such as Randi's Workaholic personality part). Just as JP, a Promoter, will create some action and excitement to get his needs met, if Randi is not having enough fun in her academic setting, she will create the fun herself. She might chat excessively with her friends, bring a CD player to school and listen to it, or make a sarcastic comment in order to get the class to laugh. Rebels are most creative when it comes to making sure that they have fun in school even if it turns out negatively. They, too, find few opportunities to get their motivational needs met in school.

Having fun is a critical need that has to be met in order for Rebels to access those parts of their personality that are necessary for success in school. This concept is often misunderstood by teachers who attempt to bribe Rebel students by promising them some fun time *after* they complete their work. If Rebels haven't already had some fun or if they don't perceive the task as fun, they have no energy to complete their schoolwork. If they are having fun, they can and will learn. For example, they can quickly memorize all the words of the latest popular song but hate to memorize spelling words and math facts that they may find boring. Musical versions of the multiplication tables can be accessed through several educational companies. In addition, students can create music and lyrics to accompany their spelling words and other subjects that require memorization. These activities could change the tasks from boring to motivating for Rebel students.

What are some of the things that Heather can do to engage Randi? Rebels like to play games and to be onstage in front of the class. Therefore, Heather might ask her to write a poem or a song about something they are studying and present it to the class. For the literature they are studying, Heather might have members of the class, including Randi, act out roles in the stories they are reading. In math class, Heather could devise competitive games in which the students move around on teams. In history, she might ask the students to write papers with the promise that if their paper meets the stated criteria, they can read it to the class. If Randi likes to tell jokes, Heather might have her read from a joke book at the start of each class.

MOTIVATING DREAMERS

The motivations of Dreamer students often seem foreign to teachers. The main motivator of the Dreamer is for some solitude during the school day. If Dreamers consistently find themselves in situations where they are required to interact in discussions, cooperative groups, or organized games, they will find ways to withdraw in order to get their required alone time. Dreamer students need their own private time and their own private space.

Because Dreamers are sensitive to the tone and nature of interactions with the teacher and other students, processing instructions and interactions take them longer than most students. They need time and space to sort themselves out before moving from listening and interacting to accomplishing written assignments. If interactions have been negative and/or critical or instructions given in a threatening manner, it will take them even longer. Dreamers are likely to have an unusual perspective and thus may start assignments from a different place than the rest of the class. Receiving criticism for this or being forced to start at the "right" place is likely to render them unable to do the assignment at all. Thus, they may "tune out" by staring out the window, make frequent trips to the bathroom or to the counselor's or nurse's office, and feign or even become ill in order not to have to go to school. Dreamers do not enjoy competition, so keeping Dreamers out of situations where their slow processing can hurt a team or group will help reduce tensions with other students. By providing Dreamers with alone time, wait time, chances to work on assignments privately, and the opportunity to pursue some aspects of the curriculum on their own, teachers will find that Dreamers often will generate some of the most imaginative, insightful, and innovative products.

MOTIVATING WORKAHOLICS

The motivators of the Workaholic are recognition for work and time structure. These activities are often inherent in school through grades, honor rolls, syllabi, and schedules. However, if these needs are not met (for example, if a teacher is disorganized or doesn't return papers), Workaholic students may overstructure, overcontrol, or attempt to make themselves look smarter than everyone else. They might criticize other students for their "stupid" answers or try to take over the group or class discussion. Ensuring that praise is given for hard work and that organizational and time structuring mechanisms are in place will keep a Workaholic on task.

MOTIVATING PERSISTERS

Persisters come to our classrooms with an already established, strong value system through which they filter everything we teach them. As their teachers, we must respect those values. Persisters also need recognition for their work, as they will work enthusiastically only at tasks that reflect their values. Usually, doing well in school is of high value to them. However, if they are not given appropriate opportunities to express their views and opinions, they can become rigid, critical, and argumentative in order to get their beliefs validated. Soliciting the ideas of Persister students and making sure that they are recognized for their high-quality work will ensure their cooperation and collaboration and make the classroom a satisfying place for them to be.

MOTIVATING REACTORS

It is essential that Reactor students know that you, as the teacher, care about them. Whether they perform at an excellent or a poor level on an academic task, they still need to know that the teacher likes them. Many teachers give recognition when high-quality work is done but forget that many students need to know that they are liked and accepted *before* they can perform well. When Reactor students do not get this need met, they are likely to feel badly about themselves, convince themselves that they are stupid, and thus do poorly in school. They may also spend their time and energy trying to get the recognition of their peers and/or the opposite sex in order to validate their worth as a person. Making sure that Reactors are recognized and complimented for their uniqueness and personality will help them feel comfortable in school so that they can do their best. They also have a need for sensory stimulation. They are more productive in an environment pleasing to their senses.

HOW TEACHERS CAN MOTIVATE ALL STUDENTS

After studying the importance of needs and incentives, the teachers in the PCM class were excited about the new information they were learning concerning the motivators for each type of student. They decided to generate a list of teacher behaviors they thought would appeal to each type of student. After seeing all the various ways they could motivate each of their students, the teachers were anxious to put these ideas into practice in their classrooms. Here are some motivation tips for different types of students:

Needs of the Workaholic: Recognize their work and provide time structure

1. Put a schedule on the board each day with times.
2. Give time warnings before it is time to change classes.
3. Devote a classroom bulletin board to students' best work.
4. Write specific positive comments on students' papers.
5. Share and let students share exemplary work with the rest of the class.
6. Call parents to let them know that students are doing a good job in school.

Needs of the Persister: Recognize their work, values, and commitments

1. Make sure that students have an opportunity to have input into the classroom rules.
2. Consistently enforce the rules.
3. Periodically ask for opinions about instructional topics and classroom procedures.
4. Publicly and privately recognize work that is well done.
5. Display exceptional work.
6. Provide opportunities for students to help others and get involved in other projects they consider worthwhile.

Needs of the Reactor: Recognize who they are and create a safe, comfortable, and attractive environment

1. Speak to students personally every day.
2. Provide opportunities for students to help each other.
3. Compliment students on unique facets of their personalities.

4. Invite students to help enhance the classroom environment.
5. Enforce classroom rules.
6. Sometimes speak in a nurturing voice.
7. Provide opportunities for students to work in groups with their friends.
8. Put stickers on students' papers.

Needs of the Dreamer: Structure assignments and provide alone time and private space

1. Don't force students to participate or sit in groups unless necessary to the assignment.
2. Allow extra time to complete assignments.
3. Make check-off lists of assignments in priority order.
4. Give wait time during classroom discussions. Teach other students the importance of wait time.
5. Make sure that expectations for assignments are clear.
6. Allow students to come in for extra help during some lunch and planning periods.
7. Provide periodic checks to ensure that written assignments are being completed.

Needs of the Promoter: Provide movement, excitement, action, and opportunities to be in the spotlight

1. Incorporate movement or hands-on activities whenever possible.
2. Stop periodically to have students do some type of movement activity.
3. Select students to help run equipment, keep score, pass out papers, and so on.
4. Provide options for students to give oral reports/answers rather than written products.
5. Provide options for projects in lieu of written work.
6. Incorporate student use of the computer when possible.
7. Use some humor.
8. Occasionally do the unexpected.
9. Develop and use game formats to reinforce concepts.
10. Challenge students.

11. Provide the rationale for rules and assignments.
12. Allow students to work independently or in groups in various areas of the room and/or stand while working.
13. Provide a structure of tangible rewards.
14. Allow students to teach the class for some subjects.

Needs of the Rebel: Provide opportunities for having fun

1. Use some humor.
2. Develop game formats for instruction and review.
3. Start the class with a joke or funny story once in a while.
4. Use comics for instruction when possible.
5. Incorporate movement and hands-on experiences when possible.
6. Do something unexpected once in a while.
7. Develop secret signals to use with some students.
8. Let students select the type of project they will do when possible.
9. Encourage students to write songs and plays to perform as projects.
10. Lecture using drawings; teach students to take notes using drawings.
11. Joke around with students periodically.
12. Stay out of power struggles.

The PCM instructor suggested that if they included something in every class, lesson, or project that would help each of the six personality types get their specific motivational needs met positively, they could head off many problem behaviors. This would result in their having more time to devote to teaching the students. This seemed more important than ever to Heather, as the required curriculum seemed to increase each year. The instructor also said that if teachers could identify and address the motivators for each type up front, they would probably not be as tired at the end of the day and would enjoy teaching more. Clearly, this would be a win-win situation.

Heather thought about how she could include something in every lesson or unit aimed at helping each of the six types get their motivational needs met positively. She had been struggling with how to get her students interested in and become critical readers of multicultural literature. Using what she had learned about motivating the various personality types, she developed the following unit. She first introduced the concept of culture to her students and had them pair up to identify the characteristics of their school culture (such as hall passes, raising hands, and so on). She reviewed the literary elements of setting and word meaning. Then she let the students select a multicultural text that would be interesting and informative to younger students with the culminating activity to present a book talk on International Night for students in the lower grades. To help students become proficient at identifying setting, she played a team game called Gnittes ("setting" spelled backward) where she called out words to see which team could be the first to determine the setting. After using the game Pictionary as an activator to show students how to use different strategies to obtain word meanings, students had an opportunity to read their selected texts. Those who had selected the same book and wanted to read with a partner were given that option. Using their knowledge of the literary aspects they had been studying, they created a two- to three-minute book talk. After rehearsing how to speak in front of an audience and giving each other feedback, they presented their book talks at International Night at their school. It was a big hit with both the parents and students.

In order to review her unit on percentages, Heather asked each student to make up a real-life problem using percentages for others in the class to solve. The students then had a choice of giving their problem to the whole class to solve, calling on volunteers to act out the problem giving the solution at the end, or acting out the problem themselves, demonstrating how they arrived at the solution. The Rebels, Promoters, and Reactors had a great time doing the acting, while the Workaholics and Promoters enjoyed being the providers of written work. The Dreamers devised the most imaginative scenarios but preferred that others act them out. All the students demonstrated that they could use percentages in real-life situations. Heather promised herself that she would consider all the personality types as she planned the activities for her lessons and units.

Educators continually strive to effectively motivate each one of their students. A great deal of teacher frustration occurs because, although many teachers succeed in motivating most of their students, there always seem to be a few in each class that seem impossible to reach. These students may be daydreaming, skipping class, socializing, coming to class high, sleeping in class, or acting out aggressively. Knowing the specific incentives for each personality type and then creating an environment where each student can get these needs met can be a key factor in managing the classroom and spending a maximum amount of time on task. As Savage (1991) points out, "Learners who feel that their needs are being met in the classroom seldom cause discipline problems because interfering with something that is meeting a need is contrary to their self-interest" (p. 39).

5

Proactive Strategies for Reducing Problem Behaviors

Key 5: Develop Intervention Strategies

As the course in Process Communication progressed, Heather developed more ideas for motivating her Rebel, Promoter, and Dreamer students. One of her class assignments was to do a case study on a student she found hard to reach. She selected JP for her case study, as he was the one who could still push her buttons and cause the most significant classroom disruptions.

In order to do her case study, Heather had to identify the student's behaviors that occurred right before classroom disruptions. She thought that if she could figure out what happened just before JP became unruly, she might have some early warning signs that trouble was coming and could head it off before it disrupted the class.

MANAGING PROMOTERS

Just before JP got out of his seat, Heather heard him talking with another student. She noticed he kept using the pronoun "you" when he was really talking about himself. She heard him say, "When you have a cell phone, you can really stay in touch with everyone all the time." As he went back to his seat, she heard him say to his friends, "When you talk to your friends, you always get in trouble." She wondered why he kept saying "you" when he really meant "I." She decided to see if he did that often. In the process, she noticed several other things he did just before they had a confrontation. She began to make a list of these behaviors. They included the following:

1. Said "you" when talking about things that he did
2. Dominated conversations
3. Frequently attempted to make deals
4. Took over even when he didn't know what he was doing
5. Got others into trouble
6. Left his seat without permission
7. Expected favors and special treatment

From the personality type descriptions, Heather figured out that JP was a Promoter. She also knew that she did not have much Promoter energy. No wonder JP was so challenging to her! She knew from her course that Promoters were motivated by action and excitement, but how could she create that in her classroom, where she emphasized structure, organization, and attention to task? However, she was determined to find ways to motivate him. She noticed that it was important to JP that he look good in front of his peers. Therefore, she sometimes selected him to be in charge of activities, such as leading the pledge of allegiance, passing out papers, or writing the homework on the board. She had observed that whenever she called on him, he immediately jumped to his feet to answer. Normally, she told him to sit down, but she thought next time she would let him stand to answer questions if he wanted to and see what happened. She also remembered that JP was able to sit quietly for only about ten minutes, and then he would start to get antsy. Therefore, she would be sure to build something active into every class, and she would change the activity often.

JP was barely passing most of his subjects. It was clear he did not like doing his class work, and he never did his homework. Heather noticed he was frequently making deals with his classmates to copy their homework or trade their lunch desserts. She also noticed that he would make bets with them, especially during competitions. One day when Heather was assigning the monthly book report, JP complained, "Book reports are a drag—why can't we do something more interesting?" Heather thought for a moment and then replied, "I have a deal for you. I'll let everyone do a project instead of a written report if they prefer. If the projects are all turned in on time and demonstrate to me that everyone read their book, we can have more project opportunities in the future." JP accepted the deal on behalf of the class, most of whom were delighted. JP talked up the project idea with the other students,

gave ideas to those having trouble thinking of a project, and made sure that everyone turned in their projects on time. On the day the projects were due, everyone had completed them! JP suggested that they share them with the class, and Heather agreed. She was surprised and pleased to see the creativity and high quality of work the students had put into their projects. She decided that she would continue to give the students choices such as this whenever possible. Because of the interest and leadership JP had shown during this time, some of his classmates began to openly admire him, and he gained positive peer status. More important, he reduced his negative behaviors in class. Heather was amazed at the change in his attitude, and she began to enjoy having him in her class.

It was obvious to Heather that JP was responding to the changes she was making. She decided to create even more opportunities in her lessons so that JP and the other students could move around. She split the class into teams in math and spelling and had competitive games because she knew that Promoters liked games and competition. JP had never liked math and was constantly creating disruptions during math class. In fact, math class was the time when

Heather had to discipline JP the most. With competition and awards added, JP showed renewed interest in math and stayed more focused on his schoolwork.

In science, Heather incorporated hands-on experiments. She also took in-class field trips where the students walked around to examine such things as the safety features and science equipment in the classroom and in-school field trips to discover the resources of the media center for their projects. She put JP in charge of collecting the write-ups of the experiments. JP was a natural leader. Whenever Heather put him in charge of anything, he made sure everyone did their work. Because of his improved status among his peers, he even began to help Heather maintain order in the classroom so that she had more time and energy to teach. These interventions worked so well with JP that Heather decided to incorporate the Process Communication concepts with other types of students. The next student she selected to focus on was Randi.

MANAGING REBELS

Heather noticed that some of the interventions she had made with JP seemed to have a positive effect on Randi as well. Identifying preliminary behaviors had worked so well with JP that Heather decided to examine the behaviors that preceded times when Randi disrupted the class. She watched Randi and picked out little things Randi said and did just before she began to act out. Heather noticed that right before Randi engaged in a confrontation, she drummed her fingers on her desk. From her class in Process Communication, Heather realized that Randi probably was starting to get bored. She wondered whether if she intervened at that moment and told a joke or said something funny to Randi she might head off the escalation. Thinking more about Randi's behavior, Heather recalled that just before Randi began drumming her fingers on her desk, she said to the boy beside her in a whiny voice, "I don't get it. What are we supposed to do?" Heather identified Randi as a Rebel and realized that these were warning signs that Randi was starting to get agitated. Heather continued to watch for antecedent behaviors over a period of several days and compiled the following list of verbal cues and actions that Randi exhibited just before she began to disrupt the class:

1. Talked in a whiney voice
2. Said, "I don't get it." "Huh." "This is hard." "The which and the what?"
3. Interrupted the class to get attention

4. Whispered to her neighbors
5. Acted as the class clown
6. Drummed her fingers on her desk
7. Passed notes to classmates
8. Doodled

Heather noticed that Randi responded positively to the team games and movement she put in her classroom activities for JP. One day, Heather saw that Randi had particular trouble paying attention during math. Armed with the knowledge that Randi needed novelty and active learning in her day to get her need for having fun met, Heather took the class out into the hall and allowed them to do their math work while lying on the floor. She noticed that Randi remained focused on her math work the entire time. As they were

walking back into the classroom, Randi thanked Heather for letting her get out of "her little box." Heather decided that she would let Randi do her math work on the floor beside her seat. However, she didn't want to draw attention to Randi, so she told the class that anyone who wanted to do their work on the floor beside their desk could do so as long as they remained on task and completed their assignments. Randi and several others jumped at the chance. Heather noticed that they concentrated on their assignment and quietly worked until they finished. From that point on, Heather sometimes allowed Randi and the other students to work in other areas of the room. Heather was amazed at how much work they did and how well behaved they were. She found it was much easier for her to manage Randi and the other students in the class when they were allowed to do their work in an environment in which they were the most comfortable.

Randi had been diagnosed as dyslexic. Although she had very high verbal skills, she had a very difficult time reading, and Heather had placed her in the slowest reading group. She kept the slower readers in the room with her, while the other reading groups went to another class for instruction. Heather noticed that when the higher reading groups returned to the class, Randi became noticeably upset, sometimes "played stupid," and acted overly silly. To offset this situation, Heather decided to have her entire reading group take a bathroom break just before the other reading groups returned to the class. In this way, Randi had a chance to move around before Heather started teaching the next subject. Everyone returned to class at the same time, and Randi stopped her negative behaviors.

Heather found that she was enjoying having Randi in her class more and more every day. She also started to notice that Randi had many strengths. Randi loved music, had a very nice singing voice, had a wonderful sense of humor, was very creative, loved writing songs and poems, had an incredible amount of energy, and was fascinated with science. Heather encouraged Randi to write songs or poems about books they were reading and about things they were studying in science. She had Randi sing her songs and read her poems to the class. In science, the hands-on activities Heather had incorporated for JP also appealed to Randi. At the end of a month, Heather reviewed Randi's behavior profile. Randi had not been confrontational once in the previous three weeks. Heather was surprised at how easy it was to manage Randi when she remembered to help her get her needs for fun and playful contact met.

MANAGING DREAMERS

Heather was still worried about Daisy. How could she help bring out the brilliance she had seen the first day of school? What were the warning signs that could tell her Daisy was in danger of being left behind? Heather noticed that just before Daisy appeared to tune out, she started talking in broken sentences. She began a thought but did not finish it. Then she began another thought and did not finish that one either. Just that morning, Heather was struck by the discontinuity when Daisy said, "The bus was . . . these lights are . . . the homework . . ." Could that be a hint that Daisy was getting on overload? Heather also noticed that Daisy had started all the class work, but she rarely completed any of it. Was this the same phenomenon as the sentence patterns that Heather had noted? She decided she would watch Daisy carefully for a week and see if there were some clues she could see that would warn her when Daisy was tuning her out.

Daisy's List of Warning Behaviors

1. Could not do more than two things at a time.
2. If given more than two assignments, she began all of them, but did not finish any.
3. Had difficulty prioritizing.
4. Spoke in disjointed, seemingly disconnected sentences.
5. Kept trying to move her chair away from her classmates.
6. Blocked her ears and closed her eyes when there was too much noise in the classroom.
7. Got a faraway look in her eyes.
8. Frequently had pauses in her speech as she appeared to search for the proper phrase.

Heather had no trouble identifying Daisy as a Dreamer. According to the notes from her class, Dreamers need their own private time and their own private space. What could Heather do to help Daisy get her need for solitude met every day? One thing would be to make sure the noise level of the class didn't get too loud. She made sure that when she reviewed the work through games and competitions that tended to get loud, she let Daisy go to the library with a specific review task to be completed. Heather also helped Daisy prioritize her

homework assignments by telling her which assignment to do first. She hoped this would enable Daisy to stay more focused on her work. She had noticed that Daisy needed more processing time when called on in class discussions, so she was rarely able to share her ideas with the class. She remembered a technique she had learned to use with students who never seemed to know the answer when they were called on. She decided to use it with Daisy. She would give Daisy some advance notice that she was going to call on her for a specific question so that she would have time to reflect on an answer. She also remembered to give Daisy wait time after asking her a question and encouraged her classmates to do the same. In addition, she encouraged Daisy to use her imagination in doing her assignments. She noticed that these techniques enabled Daisy to stay more focused on her work.

The next day, before she gave a writing assignment in English, Heather did a visualization exercise as a prompt. She encouraged all the students to use their imaginations during the visualization to help them write about something they saw in the classroom or something they did. Daisy thought and thought. Finally, she started to write. All the students except Daisy wrote an essay. Daisy wrote her story as a poem. It was titled "Visualizing the Universe." Before she read the poem, Heather tried to guess what the poem was about. Was it about an Eastern religion? Was it about the universe? Was it about nature? She read the poem and was completely taken by surprise. The poem was about swimming and was so beautiful that Heather told Daisy she would like to read it to the class and include it in the class journal. Daisy was thrilled. She timidly shared with Heather that it was the first time anything she had done in school was given value in front of her peers.

With this encouragement from her teacher, Daisy began to share her thoughts first with Heather and then with a few classmates. Daisy's ideas were often complex and very different from theirs. Those who took the time to think about her ideas began to ask her for her input on papers and projects. They stopped making fun of her because she was different and began to treat her with more respect. Daisy's self-esteem seemed to increase. Heather noticed a transformation not only in Daisy but also in the attitude of the class toward her. Because the Dreamer part of Heather's personality had the least energy of any part, she thought Daisy might be her crowning achievement for the year.

MANAGING WORKAHOLICS

Heather thought about Wesley. Usually he was no trouble at all. He was an eager learner and soaked up the information she presented as fast as she taught it. She identified Wesley as a Workaholic. It was a joy to have him in the class. She replayed the incident at the beginning of the first day when he had complained that he could not concentrate because JP and Randi were fooling around. Did Wesley give any warning signals that he was getting upset? Heather recalled that several times during that day, Wesley had used big words and overqualified his answers. She wondered if this could be a cue that Wesley was beginning to get agitated. She watched him carefully over the next few weeks and compiled the following list of behaviors that seemed to precede an angry outburst:

Wesley's List of Warning Behaviors

1. Expected himself to be perfect
2. Excessively erased his work to get it perfect
3. Took over control of a group
4. Did the work for everyone in the group
5. Complained that things were not fair
6. Called out answers
7. Verbally attacked others for not doing their share of the work
8. Got frustrated with others who did not think clearly

Heather reviewed her notes. She found that Workaholics do their best work when they are recognized for their ideas and for their accomplishments. Therefore, she devised ways to compliment him every day for things he did well. She also knew Workaholics need to know when things are due. She decided she would add time frames to her daily schedule on the board so that Wesley would know what the class was going to be doing all day long. She would also continue to make sure she gave the class a due date on all assignments.

The next morning during math class, Heather gave the class a quiz. Wesley did all the problems correctly and received an A. Heather complimented him on the great job he had done and also told him what a good mathematician he was. Heather then broke the class into teams to work on their group science projects. This was the period when Wesley usually got angry, verbally attacked his team members for not being able to think straight, and then did all the work for his team. Heather watched to see what was going to happen. To her surprise, Wesley was more cooperative with everyone. He asked for their input.

When they did not know an answer, he did not get upset but instead calmly explained things to them and gave clear, logical reasons why he wanted to do things a certain way. His team functioned very smoothly and made good progress on their project. Heather thought to herself, "It looks like helping students get their motivational needs met is one of the best ways I have found to manage a classroom."

MANAGING PERSISTERS

Heather thought about Patrick. She enjoyed having Patrick in her class. He was a very conscientious student, followed her rules, did his work, and very seldom gave her any problems. However, a couple of times, when other students did not follow the rules or did not do their share of an assignment, he did not hesitate to tell them that what they were doing was wrong. This usually ended up with the other students telling him to mind his own business and once resulted in a shoving match with JP. Heather watched Patrick for the rest of the month and noticed that just before he began verbally attacking people for not doing their share of the work, he did several things:

Patrick's List of Warning Behaviors

1. Insisted things had to be done his way
2. Said "you should" or used the words "would" or "could" in sentences
3. Inserted parenthetical expressions in his sentences
4. Pointed out that what others were doing was wrong
5. Did not credit others for things they were doing correctly
6. Became upset when others did not believe him
7. Became upset when others did not respect his beliefs

Heather recalled that Patrick, as a Persister, needed to be respected and have his opinions listened to. He also needed to be told when he was doing a good job. She decided she would ask his opinion of things periodically and also compliment him on his good work. The next morning when Patrick arrived, Heather asked him if he had heard the news that the principal had been named Principal of the Year by the Board of Education. He replied that he had. She asked him his opinion of their selection. He told her that in his opinion it was a great choice. He said the principal set high standards for the school, seemed

to know something good about every student, encouraged every student to do their best, complimented everyone on their achievements, and created a safe learning environment for every student. Heather was amazed that Patrick was so well informed and held such strong opinions about things. She noticed that he went directly to his seat and quietly began to do his work. Asking for his opinion was just the right way to start his day.

In social studies class, they were studying about the U.S. government. Heather asked the class to write a paper on why they thought the founding fathers created three equal branches of government. When the papers were handed in, she noticed it was the best paper Patrick had written all year. As she handed back his paper, Heather told him the paper was outstanding. Later she asked him if he thought having the class publish a journal giving their opinions of things they were learning about their government would help them learn more. Patrick thought that was a good idea. Heather asked him if he would be the first editor. Patrick thought everyone should have a turn being editor and agreed to be the first one. Every week they published the journal and sent a copy to the principal. The journal was very popular with the class and was a great success. Most important, Heather noted that Patrick stopped his critical and negative behaviors. From then on, Heather made certain she found something to ask his opinions about and something to praise him for every day.

MANAGING REACTORS

One day Heather noticed that in a conversation Raydia was having with another student, she kept inserting "you know" in her speech patterns in a way that interrupted the flow of her sentences and made no sense. The other student was not interested in talking with her and asked her in a sarcastic tone if she knew how to speak English. Raydia became flustered and laughed at herself in a way that Heather thought was self-deprecating. As she turned around, she spilled her water bottle all over her papers and the floor. Heather remembered that Raydia had also done this the first day of school. Knowing Raydia was a Reactor, Heather wondered if these behaviors could have been cues that Raydia was beginning to get distressed. She decided to make a list of warning behaviors for Raydia, too:

Raydia's List of Warning Behaviors

1. Said "you know" frequently
2. Laughed at herself inappropriately
3. Called herself stupid
4. Said things like, "Raydia, that was so dumb" when she made a mistake
5. Tried to please everyone
6. Had a hard time making decisions
7. Got upset when people argued near her
8. Cried when she got frustrated
9. Appeared to feel that everything that went wrong was her fault

Heather had learned that in order to do their best in school, Reactors like Raydia are motivated by praise that recognizes and accepts them for who they are. She knew she needed to let Raydia know that she liked her and not just praise her when her work was done well. She made a concerted effort to recognize Raydia's unique personality and contributions each day to see if it made a difference in her self-esteem and her performance in class. The next day when Raydia arrived at school, Heather greeted her warmly by name and told her how nice she looked. Raydia beamed with delight. Heather knew that Raydia's mother was sick, so she asked how her mother was feeling. Raydia told Heather about her mother's health and then walked calmly back to her desk.

A little later Heather called Raydia aside and told her that a student from one of the special education classes would be joining their class for math. Heather told Raydia that she knew she cared about all her classmates and wanted them all to feel comfortable in class. Therefore, she asked Raydia if she would like to be a special friend to this student and help her feel that she is a part of the class. Raydia was delighted. She invited the student to join her and her friends for lunch. She found out this student lived near her, so she made plans to walk to and from school with her.

Heather noticed that she was more successful communicating with Raydia when she asked her feelings about things. She also noticed that Raydia got very nervous whenever she had to take a test and frequently made silly mistakes on things she knew very well. She decided she would do a relaxation activity before every test to help Raydia and her classmates. She also brought some stuffed animals to school and kept them in the book corner. Before the test she would tell anyone who felt nervous that they could take a stuffed animal back to their seats to keep them company while they took the test. Raydia always took one of the animals. Interestingly, the number of silly mistakes decreased, and she rarely referred to herself as stupid.

One of the best aspects of school for Raydia was the opportunity to be with all her friends. However, she displayed anxiety about some of the subject matter. She was a good reader, she wrote well, and she liked learning about flowers and plants and animals. However, she had a very hard time in math, especially with word problems. When Heather connected word problems with people-oriented stories, they seemed not to be so daunting to Raydia. Heather was pleased that she was able to find so many ways to motivate the Reactors in her classroom.

As the year progressed, Heather realized she needed to keep the concepts she was learning in her Process Communication class in the forefront of her mind, or she tended to slip back into her favorite modes of teaching, which were lecture and discussion. The lists of warning behaviors she had made for each type provided her with clues that she needed in order to change her mode of instruction. When she noticed these behaviors, it was her cue to put more active learning, independent projects, and/or partner work into her planning in order to accommodate and motivate all the personality types in her class.

6

Thinking outside the Box

Key 6: Create a Multifaceted Environment

Heather was very pleased with the improvement in the behavior of her students and also in the improvement in their academic performance. Her enthusiasm for teaching returned, and when she saw how much her students were enjoying her classes, she was reenergized. She liked watching the lightbulbs go on as her students grasped one concept after another. She was enjoying teaching again.

She had attended a faculty meeting that day when the principal reviewed the criteria for attention-deficit/hyperactivity disorder (ADHD; American Psychiatric Association, 1994). She looked at the list:

Diagnostic Criteria for ADHD

A. Either (1) or (2)
 (1) Six or more of the following symptoms of inattention have persisted for at least 6 months to a degree that is maladaptive and inconsistent with developmental level:
  a. Often fails to give close attention to details or makes careless mistakes in schoolwork, work, or other activities
  b. Often has difficulty sustaining attention in tasks or play activities
  c. Often does not seem to listen when spoken to directly
  d. Often does not follow through on instructions and fails to finish

schoolwork, chores, or duties in the workplace (not due to oppositional behavior or failure to understand instructions)

    e. Often has difficulty organizing tasks and activities

    f. Often avoids, dislikes, or is reluctant to engage in tasks that require sustained mental effort (such as schoolwork or homework)

    g. Often loses things necessary for tasks or activities (e.g., toys, school assignments, pencils, books, or tools)

    h. Is often easily distracted by extraneous stimuli

    i. Is often forgetful in daily activities

(2) Six (or more) of the following symptoms of hyperactivity-impulsivity have persisted for at least 6 months to a degree that is maladaptive and inconsistent with developmental level:

Hyperactivity

    a. Often fidgets with hands or feet or squirms in seat

    b. Often leaves seat in classroom or in other situations in which remaining seated is expected

    c. Often runs about or climbs excessively in situations in which this is inappropriate (in adolescents or adults, may be limited to subjective feelings of restlessness)

    d. Often has difficulty playing or engaging in leisure activities quietly

    e. Is often "on the go" or often acts as if "driven by a motor"

    f. Often talks excessively

Impulsivity

    g. Often blurts out answers before questions have been completed

    h. Often has difficulty awaiting turn

    i. Often interrupts or intrudes on others (e.g., butts into conversations or games)

B. Some hyperactive-impulsive or inattentive symptoms that caused impairment were present before age 7 years.

C. Some impairment from the symptoms is present in two or more settings (e.g., at school or work and at home).

D. There must be clear evidence of clinically significant impairment in social, academic, or occupational functioning.

The treatment drug of choice is often Ritalin, which stimulates the chemicals needed to transmit messages of vigilance and nondistractibility to the brain. Side effects may include loss of appetite, insomnia, mood disturbance, tic disorder, headaches, and gastrointestinal distress.

Heather felt that she did not have any students in her class who met those criteria. However, as the principal went over the criteria, Heather realized that at the beginning of the school year, JP and Randi displayed all the symptoms on the list. This caused her to rethink what was happening with her students. Were these symptoms of ADHD behaviors that Rebels and Promoters engaged in when they were in distress because they were bored? Was it possible that helping some students get their motivational needs met positively in class could be an alternative to medication for some students? She resolved to raise this question with her Process Communication instructor at the next class. Heather was really enjoying the class. The instructor modeled the Process Communication concepts, and as a result the entire class was eager to learn more. The instructor kept their interest by varying the pace and doing many unusual things.

At the next class, Heather asked her question. Instead of answering her question directly, the instructor said he would like to do a demonstration and let the class decide for themselves. He explained that each of the personality types creates an environment in which they are most comfortable. Persisters create a Persister environment, Workaholics a Workaholic environment, Reactors a Reactor environment, Dreamers a Dreamer environment, Rebels a Rebel environment, and Promoters a Promoter environment. They also teach the way they learn. Not everyone is comfortable in all those environments or with all teaching methods. For example, those who are not like their teacher may not be comfortable in the environment the teacher creates. To illustrate this point, the teacher said that he was going to create a Rebel teaching environment. He put on a bright yellow shirt and a baseball cap that he wore sideways and added a nose ring. Then he played a punk-rock CD on the boom box at maximum volume. It was so loud that Heather could not think.

Next the teacher asked everyone to stand up and dance to the music. A few danced, but most did not. Some would not even stand up. Then the teacher asked everyone to write the names of the six personality types and the perceptions and psychological needs of each. Heather felt so uncomfortable that she could not even think of the names of one of the personality types. She began to get angry at the professor and was about to shout something at him when he stopped the demonstration and turned off the music. He asked the teachers how many of them thought they could get an A in his class. A few people raised their hands. Most did not. Then he asked how many wanted to transfer. Nearly everyone raised their hands. He told them they could not because he was the only English teacher in the building and they had to pass English in order to graduate. Several people said that they would move to another school district or another town. The instructor asked them that if for some reason their parents could not move, what would they do then. Would they be looking forward to the class as they came through the door? Very few said they would, so the instructor asked them how long before they would do something to get themselves kicked out of that class. Most of the teachers replied that it would not take long because they were at the point where they wanted to do something already.

The instructor ended this part of the demonstration by telling everyone that this is what was going on in their classrooms. Students sat there as long as they could in an environment in which they were not comfortable and then would do something to escape that environment. He concluded by saying that this could be avoided if the teachers would vary the environment periodically so that they created an atmosphere in which everyone was comfortable at least a few times every class period.

Then the instructor said he believed that those who refused to dance might have the condition known as fun-deficit/hypoactivity disorder and should be referred and tested. Perhaps once they got a diagnosis, they could get put on medication so they would be able to have some fun in his class. He said some students in his other classes were taking "fidilin," which was quite effective in enabling students to relax, have some fun, and enjoy his classes more. The teacher then posted the criteria for a diagnosis of fun-deficit/hypoactivity disorder (Kahler & Pauley, 1997).

Diagnostic Criteria for Attention-Plethora Hypoactivity Disorder (A.P.h.D.), also Known as Fun-Deficit/Hypoactivity Disorder (FDHD)

(1) Twelve (or more) of the following symptoms of Attention-Plethora Hypoactivity Disorder have persisted for at least 6 months to a degree that is maladaptive and inconsistent with developmental level.
   A. Attention
      a. Often gives close attention to details or takes care not to make careless mistakes in schoolwork, work, or other activities
      b. Often sustains attention in tasks or play activities
      c. Often seems to listen when spoken to directly

      d. Often follows through on instructions and finishes schoolwork, chores, or duties in the workplace

      e. Often organizes tasks and activities

      f. Often engages in tasks that require sustained mental effort (such as schoolwork or homework)

      g. Often has things necessary for tasks or activities (e.g., toys, school assignments, pencils, books, or tools)

      h. Often is not easily distracted by extraneous stimuli

      i. Often is not forgetful in daily activities

    B. Hypoactivity

      j. Often sits still

      k. Often remains seated

      l. Often walks rather than runs in building

      m. Often achieves excessively in situations in which it is inappropriate (in adolescents or adults may be limited to subjective feelings of perfectionism)

      n. Often has difficulty playing or engaging in leisure activities

      o. Often has his or her mind "in gear" or often acts as if the mind is "driven by a motor"

      p. Often overexplains and uses big words

(2) Some Fun Deficit Hypoactive symptoms that caused impairment were present before age 7 years.

(3) Some impairment from the symptoms is present in two or more settings (e.g., at school or work and at home).

(4) There must be clear evidence of clinically significant impairment in social, academic, or occupational functioning (e.g., count while dancing, work 18 hours a day).

    The treatment drug of choice is "Fidilin" which 1) facilitates spontaneous, creative, playful behavior; 2) inhibits postponing fun; 3) releases humor hormones; 4) enhances intimacy; and 5) reduces the guilt of "imperfect" mistakes. Side effects may include giddiness and in adults may reduce back pain and increase libido (Kahler & Pauley, 1997).

Heather realized that the instructor had reworded the criteria for attention-deficit/hyperactivity disorder to make the behaviors of Workaholics weaknesses instead of strengths.

The instructor ended the demonstration by pointing out that what were defined as negative behaviors depended on who was setting the rules and creating the environment. Everyone was okay. There was a reason for the negative behaviors. The behaviors were symptoms that the teachers and students were miscommunicating and that the students were not getting their motivational needs met.

Then the instructor referred to some of the research that had been done. He said that R. Bailey (1998) had done her dissertation at the University of Arkansas at Little Rock on this. She found that Rebels and Promoters were disproportionately represented in the following categories:

Base personality type	Percent in population	Percent labeled	Label given
Rebel	20%	55%	Difficult to teach
Promoter	5%	11%	Difficult to teach
Rebel	20%	65%	Hyperactive/impulsive
Promoter	5%	14%	Hyperactive/impulsive
Rebel	20%	52%	Inattentive
Promoter	5%	16%	Inattentive

She also found that, if a Rebel student had Promoter as the second most well developed part of her or his personality, the likelihood of his or her being labeled ADHD increased. She concluded that unique information was obtained that demonstrated that many students were referred for and consequently diagnosed ADHD as a result of behaviors that were perceived by their teachers as being hyperactive or inattentive because of a difference in personality type between teachers and their students. Bailey implied that the ability of teachers to communicate effectively with all students regardless of personality type may be the determining factor in overall student success.

The Centers for Disease Control reports that 4 to 6 percent of the U.S. population are ADHD. Yet in many schools, 30 percent or more of the students have been diagnosed with ADHD. This has become such a problem that former First Lady and current New York Senator Hilary Rodham Clinton sponsored two national conferences on the overdiagnosis of young children as ADHD. A few years ago, the Children's Hospital of the District of Columbia ran television ads on several network affiliate television stations showing children running and playing and having fun. The punch line of the advertisements was that 50 percent of the children they see who have been diagnosed ADHD have been misdiagnosed.

STYLES OF CLASSROOM MANAGEMENT

Another possible cause of miscommunication between teachers and students is the predominant management style that a teacher uses. In his book *The Mastery of Management*, Kahler (2000) describes four management styles. He identifies them as the Autocratic style, the Democratic style, the Benevolent style, and the Laissez-Faire style. Like the management tools that have been discussed in previous chapters, each of these styles is successful some of the time and not successful at other times. As we examine the strengths and weaknesses of each style, we can determine the situations in which teachers should use each of them.

The Autocratic Style

The Autocratic style might be described as the "my way or the highway" style. Teachers who use this style frequently can be heard saying things like "This is my classroom," "Things are going to be done my way. Not every student accepts that at first, but eventually they all come around," or "It's my job to clip their little wings." In this style, the teacher tells the students the classroom rules and what they are going to do and how to do it. There is very little student input. The teacher is the boss, knows more than the students, gives orders, and expects the students to carry them out. This is a very direct style and may work well in a crisis situation or with students who need direction. However, many students resent not having any input into rules they are expected to follow, and they bristle at being ordered around. Typical school examples of this style might be "These are the classroom rules," "Line up at the door and wait quietly," "No talking in the hallway," or "Do problems 1 to 10 neatly and accurately for homework tonight." Some students respond well to this style of management, but 85 percent of them respond negatively (Kahler, 1982).

The Democratic Style (also called Participatory)

Teachers who use the Democratic style frequently encourage their students to consider that the classroom is theirs. They also encourage their students to participate in devising classroom rules in the belief that if the students make the rules, they are more likely to follow them. All the students in a class should have the opportunity to participate in making decisions that affect the entire class. Everyone is encouraged to share their ideas and their work, and there is a lot of group work and cooperative learning. The teachers may make the final decision, but everyone contributes to the decisions that are made. Many students, but not all, are very productive when this style is used.

The Benevolent Style

Teachers who use the Benevolent style like to nurture their students. They treat their students as if they were all members of their family. They want all their students to feel comfortable in their classroom, and they encourage group participation in all activities. This style works well with those who need to be nurtured, but many students are not comfortable when teachers use this style. They do not have a desire to bond so closely with their classmates.

The Laissez-Faire Style

In the Laissez-Faire style, there is very little structure and minimal guidance. Students are given a goal and are allowed to find a way to achieve it with very little guidance and direction. This style encourages creativity but is a disaster for those people who need structure or direction. An example might be a chemistry teacher who gave an assignment in which he or she allowed members of the class to select a chemical element, research it, and dress as that element when they described it to the class. No further direction was given. The element they selected, the costume they designed, and the way they presented the element to the class were left up to each student. Some students enjoyed the lack of restrictions and were encouraged to be creative. Others were uncomfortable because they needed more structure.

As with the classroom management tools mentioned in earlier chapters, no one of these management styles will work with every student. Research shows that an individualistic management style is the most effective way to manage a classroom (Kahler, 1997). A teacher who uses individualistic management uses all four of the classical styles and tailors the style to the personality type that responds best to it. When teachers also then motivate each student according to their individual motivational needs, negative behaviors are greatly reduced and in many instances stop entirely.

What style works best with which students? Promoters and Dreamers respond best to the Autocratic style. Teachers have to tell them what to do in a concise, direct manner. Teachers do not necessarily have to tell them how to do something, just what to do and perhaps in what order if there are multiple assignments. Eighty-five percent of the people in North America do not respond well to the Autocratic style of management.

Workaholics and Persisters respond best to the Democratic style. They like to have their ideas and opinions considered. This style does not work well with Promoters, who tend to dominate discussions and take over groups unless they are told precisely what to do.

Reactors feel most comfortable and are most productive when teachers use a Benevolent style. They like to nurture people, and they like to be nurtured. They feel most comfortable when they are in a happy family environment. This style does not work well with Dreamers, who may feel smothered when people nurture them.

Rebels are free spirits. They do not like structure, and they hate a lot of rules. The Laissez-Faire style is for them. Give them a problem and broad parameters and then stand back and let their creative juices flow. The Laissez-Faire style does not work well with the other five types.

Dreamers, Workaholics, and Persisters need structure, Promoters and Dreamers need to be told what to do, and Reactors need to feel that they belong and are liked. All six types are most productive when teachers vary their management style so that all students are exposed to the style to which each responds best. The major disadvantage of the Individualistic style is that it requires a lot of energy on the part of the teacher, at least until the teacher becomes comfortable shifting from one style to another. However, when teachers see that when they use an Individualistic style they spend more time on instruction and less time dealing with problem behaviors and their students learn more, they usually feel that the expenditure of energy is well worth their effort. The following is an example of what this might be like.

One high school English teacher invited his class to celebrate Halloween by dressing as their favorite character from the literature they had been studying. They were also to research their character and write a brief report on him or her. Using the Laissez-Faire style of management, the teacher encouraged the students to use their creativity in designing a suitable costume for their character and in introducing their character to the class. This was all the instruction the Rebel students needed. However, these directions did not provide enough structure for the rest of the class. Therefore, the teacher used the Democratic style and asked the students to suggest things they might like to report about their character. The Workaholics and Persisters suggested that they would like to tell why they picked the character they did and report on how the character impacted the literary work.

Switching to the Benevolent style for the benefit of the Reactor students, the teacher told the students that he knew many of them were interested in people and asked them if they would like to report on some personal characteristics of the character they chose. The Reactor students really got interested in the assignment at that point and suggested that they would like to report on what their character was like and how their character related to the other characters in the work. They added that they would also like to tell how they felt about their character and the emotions they experienced when reading the work. They also asked the teacher if they could work as a group to present characters from the same work. The teacher agreed to this option.

To encourage the Dreamer imagination, the teacher told them that if they wished, they could imagine a different scenario for their character and tell how it might change the nature of the work. Finally, using the Autocratic style for the Promoters and Dreamers, the teacher also told them when the presentations were due and that presentations for individual characters were to be two minutes and for groups of characters about five minutes. This scenario demonstrates how a teacher can incorporate all the management styles into a lesson to accommodate the various personality types found in each classroom.

If teachers change the way they manage their classrooms, create different environments at various times during each class period, and individualize the way they motivate each of their students, many of the negative behaviors that students demonstrate can be stopped. Shiogi (2004), a science teacher in an inner-city high school in Los Angeles, California, completed her master's inquiry at UCLA on that subject. She determined the personality types of her students in one class, worked out intervention strategies for each of them, changed the way she taught that class by applying the concepts of Process Communication, and created different environments at various times during each class period. She also tested the motivation of each of her students by giving a pre- and posttest. She taught her other classes the way she had always taught them. She found that the motivation of the students in the experimental class increased, their grades improved, and the negative behaviors that were interfering with her teaching and their learning stopped. In her other classes, there was no increase in motivation or achievement and no reduction in disruptive behaviors. Other teachers who have applied the concepts of Process Communication in their classrooms are getting similar results: motivation, attitude, and academic achievement improve, and negative and disruptive behaviors stop or are greatly reduced (for detailed case studies, see chapters 7 and 8). In addition, teachers who use these concepts consistently in their classrooms find that they rarely have to refer students for ADHD interventions.

PART II

CHANGING NEGATIVES INTO POSITIVES

7

Differentiating for Success

One of Heather's assignments for her class on the Process Communication Model® (PCM) was to keep a journal of strategies she used to reach every type of student and record the results. She made a list of the students by name and personality type with space to record what happened as a result of her interventions. She was surprised and pleased at what happened in her classroom and was looking forward to sharing this with the other teachers in the class.

Heather had selected JP as the subject of her case study. She was eager to let the other teachers in her class know that the techniques she was using had not only changed her relationship with JP but also helped him become a more productive student. For instance, she discovered that occasionally making a deal with him, such as the one she made about the book reports (see chapter 4), seemed to get him more excited about doing his work. She made a conscious effort to put something into every class period where students could move around, such as getting into teams, finding a partner to review what was learned, and even doing a few stretches. She noticed that when she gave the students choices about their assignments, such as letting them choose whether to do an oral or a written report or to do the odd or the even math problems for homework, JP was much more likely to complete the assignment. She also allowed him to stand up when he participated in class and when doing written work. This seemed to keep him calmer. Since making these changes, Heather was happy to report that JP's work production and grades had improved and

JP and Heather

that he was not as much of a disruption in her class as he had been at the beginning of the school year. When she got to class, she found that her classmates
were just as excited as she was about sharing their strategies and successes.

DAVID'S STORY: A PROMOTER

Heather thought that one of the most impressive case studies was an example
provided by a high school teacher in a school for students who were labeled
emotionally disturbed. Every student in this teacher's class had been removed
from regular schools because of their erratic behaviors. The teacher said that
managing the class every day was the biggest challenge of her career. One
fifteen-year old boy, David, was particularly difficult. He had been in trouble
with the law since he was twelve for a variety of offenses and had served a jail
term for assault and violation of parole. He was out of jail and was court-
ordered back to school. He did not want to be in school, and the teacher was
certain that if the judge had not ordered him to school as a condition of his
release from jail, he would not have been there.

David was late to school almost every day, late to his classes, uncooperative,
and disruptive in class. He refused to do the assigned work, swore at his teach-

ers, and hit and kicked his classmates. His teachers were frustrated because they felt that they had tried everything and that nothing was working. Having learned about Process Communication, this teacher identified him as a Promoter with Rebel as his next most well developed personality part. She remembered that Promoters need action and excitement and that both Rebels and Promoters need to move around. The first thing she did was to strike up a deal with him. She said that if he did not disrupt the class for a week, she would buy him breakfast at McDonald's at the end of the week. This worked for one day. A week was too long a time for him to wait for his reward. The next deal she made was to reward him with a piece of candy whenever he made it through a whole class period without being disruptive. This worked until she ran out of his favorite candy.

She thought long and hard about how she could motivate him and reluctantly decided to change the way she taught math and history. Although this was a hard concept for her because she was a Persister, she decided to include more variety and movement in her instruction to help David get his specific needs met positively. She began to teach math by dividing the class into teams and had competition for earning points. The first team to earn five points won the contest and did not have to do any math homework that night. David responded very well to this strategy. He became energized, began to pay attention in class, and started to do his homework. Other days, the teacher allowed David to pick the homework problems. In this way, he gained status with his friends—an important consideration in dealing with Promoters. In history class, she used role playing to teach. David loved being center stage. His grades improved, and so did the grades of the other students. The teacher found it difficult to teach this way at first, but when she saw the change in David and the other students, she felt it was well worth the expenditure of energy on her part. David's other teachers reported that his behavior had improved, and she knew she had to share her strategies with them to reinforce the positive changes. Ultimately, he became a student leader and even a positive role model for the rest of the students. All his teachers were amazed at the changes in his behavior.

BERNIE'S STORY: A REBEL IN PROMOTER PHASE

A middle school teacher who taught sixth-grade history reported that she told her sixth-grade team what she had learned in the PCM class, and they discussed what they might do about Bernie, the sixth grader who was every teacher's nightmare. Bernie refused to sit in his seat, did not do any homework, swore at his teachers, hit and kicked his classmates, threw chairs, and tipped over desks. He had no interest in school and was failing every subject. He was given detention daily, had been placed in in-school suspension several times, and had been expelled from school twice. He was on the verge of being expelled again.

The members of the sixth-grade team discussed Bernie's behaviors and decided Bernie was a Rebel in a Promoter phase. Try as they might, they could not think of a single positive thing to say about him. They focused only on his negative behaviors and could see no positive strengths they could build on. The teacher asked if anyone knew what Bernie liked to do. No one knew. Finally, the guidance counselor told the group that Bernie liked to write songs. The teacher immediately said that she would have him write a song about what they were studying in history and sing it to the class. The English teacher said that he would have him write a song about what they were studying in English. The team thought that might be too similar to what he was doing in history, so they asked the English teacher to come up with a different way to stimulate Bernie's interest. The English teacher decided to have the students act out the stories they were reading. In a few weeks, the class was going to start a segment on poetry, and eventually they would be writing their own poems. He decided to use Bernie's interest in writing songs to stimulate his interest in poetry. He would ask Bernie if he would like to try setting some of the poems they were reading to music. When they started to write their own poems, he hoped that Bernie would see the connection between poetry writing and songwriting and would be more willing to take a chance at writing his own poems.

The science teacher used to do demonstrations in front of the class and have the students write up the results. Although she was a little nervous about this at first, she thought if she included more hands-on experiments that the students could do themselves, Bernie might become more focused. One day Bernie came to her and asked if he could write a song about the experiment he just did. Naturally, the science teacher agreed. The teachers carried out their plans, and over time Bernie's attitude toward school changed. He stopped his acting-out behaviors in his classes, he began doing his homework, and his grades went from Ds and Fs to Bs and Cs. The teachers were delighted, Bernie's parents were thrilled, and the principal was happy to see the transformation.

JOSH'S STORY: A REBEL IN A PROMOTER PHASE

The next case study presented was about Josh, a third grader who was coded learning disabled. In addition to having difficulties reading, he was noncompliant, displayed oppositional and inappropriate behaviors, teased his peers, manipulated both peers and adults, interrupted class, called out in class using inappropriate language, and refused to participate in classroom and playground activities. The school team was considering adding the code of emotionally disturbed to his disability. From what his teacher had learned in the PCM course, she concluded he was a Rebel in a Promoter phase. She knew the types of student who had the most difficulty in schools and classrooms were those with high Rebel and Promoter energy. In their PCM class, the teachers had discussed a number of activities that appealed to Rebels and Promoters, so she decided to implement some of these. The teacher thought that Josh would enjoy some group games on the playground. She decided to teach him the rules before she taught them to the other students and then have Josh help her explain them to the class. This activity lent itself to his becoming one of the group leaders for the games they played. She used reinforcements that were meaningful to him. For example, he liked to buy things from the Teacher Store. Therefore, the teacher made a deal with him. For compliance in a group setting, she rewarded him periodically with a Teacher Token, which could be used to buy items in the Teacher Store. Within a five-week period, his positive participation in classroom and playground activities increased from 10 to 50 percent per day.

RAMUNDO'S STORY: A PERSISTER

Ramundo's fourth-grade teacher described him as a student to whom rules and routines were very important. He was always the first one to point out when the schedule wasn't updated and had a great need to be respected. He also got offended easily. He displayed a great deal of pride in his Hispanic heritage and was quick to point out that his parents spoke perfect English. He also frequently complained indignantly if someone made derogatory comments about him or his family. Fairness was very important to him, and he got emotionally charged when confronted with perceived injustices. If a rule was not upheld universally, he obsessed on the unfairness of the situation. He had become overly suspicious of adults whom he believed to be acting unfairly against him. He reacted quite negatively to instances where a teacher singled him out in a group situation for a behavioral issue. His teacher did not have any trouble identifying Ramundo as a Persister.

One of the situations that the teacher wanted to work on was Ramundo's argumentative behavior. She began to start interventions with phrases such as "I respect the fact that you have a different opinion" or "I understand your beliefs about this situation." She listened carefully to him and validated his opinions. When he complained about another student or adult, she started off by telling him, "I hear your concern, and thank you for telling me about this." When he complained about the unfairness of a situation, she asked his opinion about what could be done.

These interventions began to work. Ramundo became noticeably calmer and looked less threatened when he came to school each morning. He developed better relationships with his teacher and the other adults in the school. He seemed less stressed and more responsive to both social and academic interactions with adults and other students. She realized that he had a lot to offer, and she was going to continue to find ways to give him positive recognition in the classroom.

LAVERNIA'S STORY: A REBEL

A first-grade elementary school teacher reported that she had a very bright girl in her class who was struggling with her spelling. She had been diagnosed with dyslexia, was having trouble reading, and could never remember how to spell any of her vocabulary words. In addition, she was very energetic, ran everywhere she went, and liked to jump around. The other students began to make fun of her in spelling, and she would react by spitting on them or hitting them. The teacher identified Lavernia as a Rebel. She knew that as a Rebel, Lavernia needed to have fun. The teacher's challenge was how to make spelling fun for Lavernia. One day on the playground, the teacher saw her imitating a cheerleader leading cheers. She wondered if Lavernia would remember how to spell the words if she could spell them in a cheer. She decided to experiment and see. She asked Lavernia if she could figure out a cheer for three of her spelling words for homework and then do the cheers for the class the next day. To her surprise and joy, Lavernia spelled the words right. The teacher enlisted the aid of Lavernia's parents and had them watch Lavernia spell all her vocabulary words as cheers every night. The teacher let her do several cheers a day for the class and found that this also benefited some of the other students. Almost immediately, Lavernia started to get 100 percent on her spelling tests. Her classmates stopped teasing her about her poor spelling, and Lavernia stopped her acting-out behaviors. This enabled the teacher to spend less time managing Lavernia's behavior and more time teaching subject matter.

SARAH'S STORY: A WORKAHOLIC

Next, a seventh-grade teacher reported about a student named Sarah who had been diagnosed as developmentally disabled and who constantly sought a great deal of reassurance. She was eager to participate in class, worked very hard, did all her work on time, and in many ways was a very good student. However, her need for constant reassurance that she was doing a good job resulted in many interruptions during the class. She also kept leaving her seat, thereby interrupting small groups the teacher was meeting with. To get her to change this behavior, the teacher tried several interventions. First, the teacher sat Sarah down front, where the teacher could monitor her more closely. However, because she was closer to the teacher, she got out of her seat more often to tell the teacher something. The teacher then used verbal reminders that Sarah should stay in her seat. This did not work either.

The teacher believed that Sarah was a Workaholic and that she had strong Reactor and Promoter parts of her personality as well. The teacher devised a system whereby she gave Sarah several extra-credit tickets at the beginning of class. Every time Sarah got out of her seat without permission, the teacher took one of the extra-credit tickets away from her. Those she had left at the end of the class period she got to keep and could use for extra credit on her papers. Sarah liked the idea of getting higher marks on her assignments and took pride in keeping all her extra-credit tickets. She would count them and tell everyone in the class how many she had. Within a few days, she was staying in her seat almost for the entire class period. She had greatly reduced the number of inappropriate interruptions, and she had stopped shouting out the answers to questions without raising her hand. This resulted in the other students getting more work done and the teacher being able to maintain the focus of her lessons.

KIM'S STORY: A REBEL IN A PROMOTER PHASE

One of the more interesting case studies to Heather was an eighth-grade boy named Kim, who was a Rebel in a Promoter phase. The thing Kim did that concerned his teacher and prevented him from completing his work was that he quit doing his assignments when he got angry or thought he might look bad in front of his peers. When things did not go his way or when people would not do what he wanted, he would shut down and become vengeful. He also tended to get others off task and would try to get the teacher to solve problems for him. He refused to do any of his assignments and was well on the way to failing his eighth-grade year. The teacher concluded from his behaviors that he was a Rebel in a Promoter phase and needed excitement, action, and fun. Being a Persister in a Workaholic phase herself, she had to think a long time before she could come up with something that fulfilled these criteria. Finally, she thought of something. She knew that he had his own dirt bike, loved to ride it, and loved to go to motorcycle races. She made a deal with him. She told him that if he did all his homework, turned it all in, and got a 3.0 or higher on his next report card, she would take him to a motorcycle race. Kim loved the deal. He turned in all his homework for the grading period, and all of it was done correctly. He also got a 3.2 on his report card. Although the teacher could not continue to take him to motorcycle races, they had established a good relationship through this "deal." As a result, Kim started to work for this teacher. He liked her, and through getting to know Kim and his talents and interests, the teacher began to genuinely like him as well and to concentrate on his strengths.

KAREEM'S STORY: A PROMOTER

Next, a middle school teacher reported on her eighth-grade student Kareem. She described a long list of his behaviors that had been irritating her, including fidgeting all the time, having a caustic remark for every occasion, being disorganized, and not completing assignments. He displayed poor writing skills, had frequent verbal outbursts during class, and was constantly out of his seat. He was also very persuasive and frequently talked other students into joining him in his negative behaviors. He was definitely a Promoter. She knew she needed to include more active tasks in her lessons if she was going to reach Kareem. First, she moved his seat to the front of the class so she could intervene quickly. When he acted out, she found she was able to get him back on task with "the look." She knew that, like most Promoters, he was interested in money. Therefore, she shared with him that the school system was paying $5,000 a year to educate each student. This impressed him. When he began to act out, the teacher would ask him privately in a casual manner if he thought the school system was getting its $5,000 worth. That usually brought him back on task. She also told him she thought that he was probably one of the smartest students in the class and that if he applied himself, he could do very well. She felt confident that no one had every told him that before. When his grades started to improve, she attributed it to more time on task and increased self-esteem.

She gave him jobs like passing out papers and keeping score during games. During reading assignments, she decided to allow members of the class to move around to different locations within the classroom to do their reading. He seemed to enjoy this and began to complete more of his reading assignments. She also gave him occasional one-on-one attention and gave him clear directives concerning his assignments. He completed his work and began to ask for help when he needed it. His grade went from C to A in her class.

JANICE'S STORY: A REBEL

A ninth-grade high school teacher reported a litany of behaviors from his student Janice, who constantly spoke out of turn, was easily distracted, fidgeted, was unable to sit still, blamed others, slammed her books on the ground, and left her seat without permission. The teacher was just about to ask the administration to remove this student from his classroom when he took the PCM course as a last resort. After learning about personality types, he immediately identified Janice as a Rebel. He learned that Rebels need to have some fun in class in order to be able to think clearly. Although this was a completely new idea to him, he decided to include jokes in his lessons or to show cartoons to kick off a lesson. He also incorporated stretch breaks. He gave Janice a leadership role from time to time when playing intellectual games, created a fun mood in class, and incorporated creative activities such as creating comic strips to summarize readings. Janice seemed to be more energized. She became more focused on her schoolwork and appeared to be much more stimulated in class. Since she was in his first period class, he gave her the role of leading the pledge to the flag in the morning and reading the daily announcements to the class. Janice always ad-libbed something funny when she read the announcements. This started the day off on a positive note for everyone. The teacher noticed that her negative behaviors were greatly reduced, and her grades began to improve.

RICHARD'S STORY: A DREAMER

A fourth-grade elementary school teacher reported that she was frustrated with a Dreamer student, Richard. She knew he was smart, but he was not working up to his potential. He never caused any problems in class, but he was inattentive, daydreamed, and generally tuned her out. In addition, he had problems at home. He had very little adult supervision and received almost no help doing his homework. He completed little class work, he never completed his homework assignments, and was not doing well on tests. The teacher explained to him that his incomplete assignments were contributing to his not doing well on tests. She explained to him that completed assignments were the key to success or failure in school. She started to meet with him privately at the end of each day to delineate his homework assignments and to prioritize them for him. Soon he was completing his homework assignments accurately. Because she knew Dreamers needed some solitary time in order to function at their best, she found ways to allow him to work alone several times each day. She also gave him only one or two things to do at a time. As a result of these interventions, she found that he paid much closer attention during instruction and completed more assignments, and his grades showed significant improvement.

JEROME'S STORY: A REBEL IN A PROMOTER PHASE

The next story was from a first-grade teacher who shared information about Jerome, a student in her class who had special needs. A major problem was that most of Jerome's communication was through aggression. He also found it difficult to focus, stay on task, and follow directions. He disrupted the class an average of fifteen times per class period by throwing temper tantrums. He was coded as language delayed, and the school team was going to recommend that he be placed in a special class. As the teacher observed him so she could report on his behaviors at the next school team meeting, she realized that he was a Rebel in a Promoter phase. At the meeting, she requested that before he was placed in a special class, she be allowed to try some interventions with him and report back to the team in a month. The parents and the team agreed. Working closely with the speech/language pathologist in the school, the teacher developed a picture communication book for transitions. She learned about social stories that feature the student as the main character behaving appropriately in various situations, and she started using them to teach him social skills such as greeting his friends appropriately and asking them to play at recess. During his speech time, he got a chance to practice the scripts in private and then act them out in a controlled setting. She reinforced appropriate behavior with things that were meaningful to him. When he interacted with others correctly without tantrums, he was given ten minutes to play with an educational game of his choice plus a good-job sticker. After he received ten good-job stickers, his parents took him to McDonald's. Within five weeks, the number of temper tantrums was reduced to an average of fewer than eight per day.

JUAN'S STORY: A REBEL

Next to report was a seventh-grade middle school social studies teacher whose Rebel student, Juan, was driving her crazy. He was creative and liked to have fun, and he was frequently off task, which meant that he accomplished little or no work in class. He became easily frustrated, got angry whenever things did not go his way, was negative, and complained constantly. Because this teacher had several Rebels in her class, she decided she would implement a variety of strategies to try to motivate them. First, she made a deal with the entire class. If everyone remained on task for an entire period, she would let them socialize for the first five minutes of the next class. In addition she gave a two-minute stretch break in the middle of the class period asking the students to take turns leading the stretches. She began using more games and hands-on materials to diversify her teaching techniques. When she assigned a long-range project, she let the students work in groups to design and present the projects. She found that these strategies worked well for all her students, especially the Rebels. The results of her case study showed that Juan stayed on task longer and did more of his work, and, best of all, his grades and test scores improved. He was no longer a major management problem for his teacher. In fact, she even began to enjoy having Juan in her class.

HUBERT'S STORY: A PERSISTER

An eleventh-grade high school teacher reported on his student Hubert, who had strong opinions about everything and believed that he was always right. Hubert was sarcastic, argumentative, and physically aggressive with teachers and students who disagreed with him. He was strong and had already hurt some of his classmates and one teacher. As a result, he had spent a term in Juvenile Hall. From what his teacher had learned in the PCM course, he concluded that Hubert was a Persister who needed to be respected, to be told when he did a good job, and to have his opinion sought. The teacher began greeting Hubert at the door every day and asking his opinion about how things were going. Hubert responded by entering the room smiling and was prepared when the class started. During class discussions, the teacher asked Hubert's opinion whenever he could, thanked him for his opinion, and told him how much he valued the fact that he provided the class with a different angle about topics. Hubert's attitude began to change from being hostile to being more cooperative. He began to volunteer to do things. He offered many excellent ideas in discussions. He became a class leader and put forth 100 percent effort in his class work. As a result, his grade improved in that class, and he ceased to be a management problem for the teacher. However, he continued to exhibit negative behaviors in his other classes, where these techniques were not used.

SHERRY'S STORY: A REBEL IN A PROMOTER PHASE

Sherry's teacher was at her wit's end. He reported to the group that when she was interested in what she was doing, Sherry was creative, playful, and charming. However, Sherry could just as easily be sarcastic, refuse to do assignments she did not want to do, become combative, and instigate fights in his fourth-grade class. The teacher concluded that Sherry was a Rebel in a Promoter phase. Knowing as the other teachers in the class did that this was a difficult combination, the first thing he decided to do was make sure that Sherry had an active class job. He remembered that when he had asked Sherry to pass out papers or straighten the bookshelves, she really seemed to enjoy this. Therefore, he let her select from a list of jobs. She chose to keep the shelves straight. He also initiated a system whereby she could earn rewards for appropriate behavior. Sherry enjoyed this positive attention and greatly reduced her negative interactions in the classroom. She began to offer to do extra work like helping organize the room and clean the bookshelves. The positive relationship that developed because of these interactions resulted in less refusal to do work and a reduction in power struggles between the teacher and student. Both ended up with a greater appreciation for each other.

CINDY'S STORY: A REACTOR

Cindy was a Reactor student in eleventh grade. One of her teachers described Cindy as a student who kept insulting herself and putting herself down, was indecisive, questioned her ability to do anything, and was not getting any of her work done. She also acted confused and asked for clarification of things that her teacher was sure she already knew how to do. She constantly looked for validation. The teacher had learned that Reactors need support for who they are and are keenly aware of their sensory environment. Therefore, he decided to meet her with a friendly smile and greet her by name every day when she came into class. Cindy responded with a big smile and walked more confidently to her seat. The teacher had learned that Reactors like to be help-ful. Because of her excellent handwriting, he asked her to help him from time to time by writing the daily homework assignments on the board. He also asked her to be a peer tutor for someone who had missed two weeks of class. As a peer tutor, her leadership skills began to emerge, and she started showing her competence without the confusion she had previously demonstrated. Her teacher also asked her advice about the room arrangement and bulletin boards and used some of her ideas. This was a particularly effective strategy because she was recognized for her strength areas. Cindy was obviously feeling more comfortable in the class and stayed focused on her schoolwork. Soon her grades began to improve, reflecting the change in her attitude.

ROGER'S STORY: A WORKAHOLIC IN A PERSISTER PHASE

Roger was a thirteen-year-old eighth grader who had been diagnosed with a speech and language disability requiring the services of a speech therapist twice a week. He had a very highly developed sense of right and wrong and was a stickler for following the rules. He was fairly rigid about having things done the way he believed they should be, and whenever he didn't get his own way, he became so frustrated that he would shut down and cry. When things were going his way, however, he was a good student who always did his work accu-rately and on time. He also liked to be in charge of group projects. However, it was difficult for him to delegate assignments when working in a group. He was impatient with the others and had a tendency to end up doing all the work himself so that it would be up to his standards. He usually completed his schoolwork early, and he also enjoyed and was very good at computer games. In class, he tended to blurt out answers without raising his hand. The teacher concluded he was a Workaholic in a Persister phase. She realized she needed to give him recognition for his neat and accurate work. She also knew that Workaholics like to know exactly when all assignments are due. She found his most distracting characteristic was his tendency to blurt out answers without raising his hand. This bothered her because it prevented other students from having a chance to answer questions, and sometimes it disrupted her train of thought. She spoke with him about it and worked out an arrangement whereby he would self-count the number of times he did this. She gave him a reward of added computer time for improvement. With the self-tally, the student became aware of the actual number of times he was blurting out the answers. He consciously made an effort to raise his hand and worked hard for his extra computer time. The teacher used a prearranged hand signal to acknowledge when he had his hand raised. This signal let the student know the teacher was aware he knew the answer even if he was not called on. Both the hand signal and the added computer time were ways for the teacher to give the student recognition for the effort he was making to reduce the number of times he blurted out the answers. After five weeks, he had significantly reduced the number of times he called out, thereby making it easier for the teacher to continue her instruction. This helped everyone have more of an opportunity to participate.

ALBERT'S STORY: A PROMOTER

The same teacher reported on her easily identifiable Promoter student Albert, who lied, stole, made noises, ridiculed others, and pushed the envelope to see how much he could get away with. These behaviors left little time for him to complete any academic tasks. He fidgeted in class, made fun of other students, and broke or bent every classroom rule. She changed his seat to put him near her so she could intervene more quickly, but this was only marginally effective. Reflecting on the intervention she had used with Roger, she decided to institute a similar strategy with Albert. However, she realized that if she was to be instrumental in helping Albert change his behaviors, she had to give him a personal challenge, so she presented the idea to him in the form of a deal. She told him to self-tally the number of times he made a noise and gave him a reward of more computer time for improvement. The self-tally made the student aware of how many times he actually was making noises. He turned it into a personal challenge to reduce the number of times he did this. The teacher found a picture of a computer and cut it into pieces. He was awarded a piece of a computer for every fifteen minutes he went without making a noise. When the picture was complete, he was rewarded with ten minutes of computer time. Albert responded positively to the challenge, liked the idea of the deal, and even enjoyed putting the puzzle pieces together. The teacher also broke down his assignments into smaller components and set time limits for the student to complete each part. Albert considered this a competition and usually finished before the time limit. Work completion significantly improved, and so did his grades.

HEATHER'S REFLECTIONS

Heather was captivated by the presentations and interventions. She was struck by the realization that every personality type was evident at every grade level and in both genders. Another thing she noticed was that many times the same interventions worked with different personality types. For instance, being selected as a peer tutor had a positive effect on Reactors because of the helping aspect, on Promoters because of the elevated status, and on Workaholics and Persisters as a worthwhile task in which to engage.

Using a contract or token system had appealed to Workaholics when earning extra credit, to Promoters when earning rewards as the result of a deal, and to Rebels as a way to have fun. Most of the students responded well to stretch breaks, hands-on activities, role playing, games, and leadership roles. Both Dreamers and Promoters benefited from having their assignments broken down into small parts. Getting students involved in monitoring their own behavior was positively viewed by Promoters as a contest, by Persisters as an awareness-raising exercise, and by Workaholics as a task to manage.

As Heather left the class that day, she thought that perhaps implementing workable interventions with students exhibiting problems was not going to be as difficult as she thought once she learned to identify their personality types. She realized that if she would put something in each class to motivate each of the six personality types, she would simplify her classroom management.

Dealing with Acute Negative Behaviors

Throughout this book, we have been dealing with classroom management strategies to head off conflict before it arises. However, there may be times when, despite a teacher's best efforts, some students will still display negative behaviors. In previous chapters, we examined some of the causes of these behaviors, such as students not getting their motivational needs met positively, differences in personality type between teachers and students, teachers creating only one learning environment or using only one interaction style, and teachers using only their favorite means of communicating with their students and not shifting to the students' frame of reference.

All these are things teachers can impact by changing the way they manage their classroom. However, many times students' behaviors are the result of things that have happened outside class and will have nothing to do with the teacher. For example, the students might be angry or depressed about something that happened at home, on the way to school, in another class, or in the school hallways, and as a result they may display behaviors that will be challenges for the teacher. What can teachers do to facilitate resolution of the conflict?

First of all, teachers must understand that they cannot "make" people feel good and behave well. They can only provide opportunities for this to occur. Neither can they "make" them feel bad. The decision whether to feel good or feel bad belongs to the person (Kahler, 1982). However, because of their own beliefs, teachers may inadvertently add to or further student distress. Consider the following four myths identified by Kahler (1978), which he postulates to be the underlying justifications for furthering distress (miscommunication):

1. "I believe I can *make* you feel good emotionally."
2. "I believe you can *make* me feel good emotionally."
3. "I believe I can *make* you feel bad emotionally."
4. "I believe you can *make* me feel bad emotionally."

The teacher who believes myth 1 will overgive and overdo for his or her students. This is a negative form of rescue that reinforces over-adaptive, nonproductive behavior. For example, when giving a student another chance at doing a problem correctly, a teacher might say, "Let me help you. That will *make you feel* better." Telling the student, "This will make you feel better" conveys the message that other people are responsible for making a person feel good emotionally. If the student does not feel good, he or she may blame the teacher, and this may lead to unproductive student behavior.

The teacher who believes myth 2 will overpersonalize the situation in an attempt to motivate. They might say something like "Oh, you *make me* so proud" or "You've *made me* so happy." Although these comments may seem harmless, the message sent is that "my good feelings are dependent on you/your behavior." If students accept this message, they may think/feel that they are responsible for the teacher's feelings.

The teacher who believes myth 3 will use frustrated, righteous anger or vengeful, vindictive anger to threaten or manipulate students into "appropriate" behavior. These maneuvers only result in more negative behaviors over time. They may be overheard saying something like "You are hopeless" or "You are as dumb as a rock."

The teacher who believes myth 4 will use the emotional blackmail of guilt to "motivate" his or her students. "You *hurt my feelings* so bad when you did that." Or "Why do you want *to upset me* so much?" These types of statements encourage others to believe they have the power over the teacher's feelings and are often designed to "make them feel guilty" and thereby stop the unwanted behavior. People do not make long-term, positive changes from this kind of "guilt trip."

DEALING WITH NEGATIVE BEHAVIORS

Although we cannot "make" people feel good and behave well, we can "invite" them to do so by inviting them out of distress. The most effective way to deal with students' negative/distress behaviors is to help them get the motivational need(s) of their personality phase met positively (Kahler, 1982).

Rebel in Severe Distress

Let's suppose that one day Randi's father physically abused her at home just before she came to school because she would not do something he told her to do. She walked into Heather's classroom looking for a fight. When Heather said good morning to her and offered her a high five, Randi, instead of responding with a high five, swore at Heather, refused to sit in her seat, shoved her chair into the wall, tipped over her desk, and picked a fight with Patrick. What could Heather do?

According to Kahler (1982), when people show this degree of distress, it is the best indicator of the current phase of their personality. (See chapter 1 for a discussion of phase.) Most of the time when this happens, they are letting us know that the motivational needs of their phase are not being met. Therefore, rather than take this affront personally, Heather can remember several things to help her deal with the situation. First and foremost, there is a reason that Randi is acting the way she is that has nothing to do with anything Heather has done. Heather needs to confirm with herself that Randi is still a good person even when her behavior is unacceptable. It is very important that Heather not accept Randi's "invitation" to join her in distress by retaliating or becoming upset with her, as this would escalate the conflict. If Heather can understand that Randi is displaying the behaviors of a Rebel in severe distress, she can address the motivational need of Rebels, which is playful contact.

To deal effectively with this situation, Heather needs to approach Randi in a playful way. This is counterintuitive to what most teachers would naturally do in this situation and may not be easy. It may require Heather to use a lot of energy. However, if Randi remains in distress, she may end up being expelled from school. Heather believes that expelling students from school is an easy "solution" that does not help them address their problem or participate in learning. She feels her job is to do everything she can to keep them in school so that they have a chance to succeed in life. For this reason, she decided she would make every effort to reach Randi (and all her other students) before she referred anyone for suspension or expulsion.

Heather's first concern was to stop the fight with Patrick. She walked up to Randi and in a joking manner, said, "Ouch, that hurt. Hey, Randi, this is your desk talking. That really hurt my back when you knocked me over." Randi stopped arguing with Patrick and stared at Heather as she continued talking, this time as if she were the chair. "Yeah, Randi. My back hurts too. I didn't know you could shove me that hard. Very impressive! Skidding across the floor was kinda cool, but the crashes are tough on the back. You ever been shoved against a wall? Ouch! If you're gonna do that very often, I guess I better practice braking so I don't get hurt when I crash." Randi started to smile. Then she started to laugh. She apologized to the chair and the desk and told them that her father had shoved her up against the wall at home, so she knew how they felt. Heather continued pretending to be the chair as she was talking with Randi and told her she'd like to continue their conversation after class. Randi, still talking to the chair, agreed.

Heather knew that Rebels like mechanical toys. Therefore, several weeks before she had purchased some robots that she thought she would use in a sci-

ence demonstration. She figured that this was the time to use them. She had preplanned a science demonstration to introduce the robots to the class. As the other class members filed into the room, Heather took out the robots and showed the class how they worked. The robots were a great success with everyone. Randi was especially intrigued. The crisis passed. Heather breathed a sigh of relief. She was amazed at how well these interventions worked. Randi was still in class and was doing her schoolwork. At the first opportunity, Heather reported the abusive father to the appropriate school authorities.

Reactors in Severe Distress

Later that day, Heather noticed that Raydia seemed to be depressed. Physically, she was in the classroom, but it was obvious that her mind was elsewhere. She repeatedly made silly mistakes all day long. As she was getting out of her seat, she dropped her binder and her papers, and supplies spilled out all over the floor. At that point, she burst into tears, and through her sobs, Heather heard her say, "I hate myself." Heather made several attempts to tell Raydia how nice she looked and how much she enjoyed having her in class, but Raydia was not listening. As Raydia was leaving the classroom, she asked Heather if she could talk to her for a minute. Heather agreed. When they were alone, Raydia confided to Heather that she was pregnant and did not dare to tell her parents. She had even considered suicide as the only way to resolve her situation. Heather was surprised but did not let it show. She knew that she had to deal with Raydia's distress before Raydia could even hear what she was saying.

Fortunately, Heather had a free period, so she asked Raydia if she would like to stay in her classroom and join her for a soft drink. Raydia agreed. Heather encouraged Raydia to talk about anything she wished, and they talked for nearly an hour. After a few minutes, Raydia was not exhibiting as much distress, and she was able to calmly tell Heather all the details, including the fact she was afraid her father would kick her out of the house. Heather heard her out, reassured her that she was still a good person, and suggested that Raydia go with her to talk to the guidance counselor. Raydia agreed. Heather accompanied her to the guidance counselor and explained the situation to him in very sympathetic terms. She then went to brief the principal. The counselor was able to convince Raydia to tell her parents in his presence. Heather later learned that, to everyone's surprise, Raydia's parents were supportive and helped her make a decision about what to do.

Persisters in Severe Distress

Another day, Patrick was very angry when he came into class. His teacher in the previous class had given them an assignment to write a story and suggested that they use their imaginations in writing it. Patrick lived on a farm and had several hundred chickens, so he decided to write about chickens. Using his imagination, he wrote that one of the chickens was three feet tall. When he read his story to the class, the teacher ridiculed him for saying a chicken could be three feet tall. The other students began to laugh at him and to make fun of him. Patrick defended what he had written and reminded the teacher in a sarcastic tone that she had told them to be creative. However, when the students continued to make fun of him, he unleashed a barrage of verbal abuse at them. He even got into a shoving match with JP.

He was still very angry when he came into Heather's classroom, and every time anyone said anything to him, he continued to be sarcastic and verbally abusive. Heather was not aware of what had happened in the other class, but this was so out of character for Patrick that she knew something serious had happened that had triggered this outburst. She picked up a stack of papers and walked over to Patrick's desk. She told him that he had written an outstanding essay on China and that she was impressed by the logical way he had presented the information to support his opinions. She asked him if he would be willing

to read his paper to the class. At first, he was reluctant to do so. He told her that he did not care whether his classmates heard his opinions. However, when Heather told him that she wanted to use his paper as the focus of a discussion, he agreed. He read the paper and led the class discussion. Most of his classmates stopped teasing him, and he continued to do high-quality work in Heather's class. Interestingly, he lost respect for the other teacher, lost interest in the other teacher's class, and did just enough work to get a passing grade.

Promoters in Severe Distress

JP never did stop teasing Patrick about the chicken. He would walk up to Patrick in the hall and crow like a rooster or cluck like a chicken. One day, Patrick made a sarcastic response and belittled JP. The barbs flew back and forth, and Patrick was getting the best of the exchange. As they entered Heather's room, JP punched Patrick in the back of the head. Heather did not see the punch, but she saw Patrick stagger as he entered the room and heard him swear at JP. She asked Patrick what happened, but he did not answer her. She told JP to tell her what happened, and JP told her Patrick tripped coming into the room. Patrick called JP a liar and moved to hit him. Heather stepped between Patrick and JP. She very calmly suggested to Patrick that he return to his seat and write out a brief explanation of everything that had happened. She told him that after he finished, she would like to discuss his view of the situation with him. She told JP to go to the computer lab and write out a brief explanation of what happened. Later, after she read both sides of the story, she praised Patrick for his creative idea of a three-foot-tall chicken as well as his willingness to share his essay on China with the other students.

Later she took JP aside and suggested they make a deal. JP looked at her quizzically and said, "Tell me your deal, Teach." Heather replied, "Instead of you sitting in class today, go to the computer lab and pull up some of my work for our lab tomorrow. I'll give you my science disk and a hall pass. Look at what I've got prepared for tomorrow and come up with ways to punch it up and make it more interactive for the class. If you do a good job, I'll give you extra credit and a free pass from my class to be used whenever you want, except on test days. Deal?" JP replied, "Sure, Teach! What's the catch?" Heather replied, "No catch, just a deal. You must agree that you will never interact negatively with Patrick again. In fact, you will develop a special part in tomorrow's lab for him. Deal?" Without looking at Heather, JP agreed. Heather continued saying, "Look me in the eye and let's shake on it." JP shook hands and agreed to the deal.

Because JP had just gotten his need to feel special met positively and because he was being allowed to gently bend the rules, he was honor bound to fulfill his end of the bargain. He went one step further and made sure Patrick was the star in the next day's lab. Because he exceeded the expectations of the deal, he did not have to feel beholden. This was a win-win situation for everyone. Heather won because she found a way to resolve the conflict, Patrick won because he had a leadership role in the lab, and JP won because he was "The Man."

Dreamers in Severe Distress

The week everyone dreaded had arrived. The class had to begin taking the high-stakes tests that were mandated under the No Child Left Behind Act. The first day's test was multiple choice and it was timed. Heather knew that Daisy did not do well on multiple-choice tests because she saw so many possibilities that she had great difficulty picking one right answer. Right in the middle of taking the test, Daisy got up and went to the bathroom. She did not return. Near the end of the test period, Heather told the other test monitors that she wanted to check the girls' bathroom to make sure Daisy was all right. When she got there, she found that physically there was nothing wrong with Daisy, but psychologically she was stressed out. Daisy refused to return to the classroom. Because the testing period was over, Heather told Daisy she did not have to return. Instead, she gave her a hall pass and suggested that she go to the school library for the next class period and read about something that interested her. Heather told her that they would be writing a poem in English class later in the day and suggested she might want to think about a possible topic. She also asked Daisy if she could stay after school for a few minutes because she would like to explore what she could do to help Daisy succeed on the mandated tests. Daisy went to the library, where she was able to reflect peacefully on the day's events and the problem she had with multiple-choice tests. She also thought about several topics she would like to write poems about and started writing one. When Heather and Daisy met after school, Heather talked to Daisy about how much she appreciated and valued her depth and imagination when expressing her ideas, especially in writing. She explained that in this case, getting the test done is more important than doing it deeply and imaginatively or exploring all the possibilities in each answer. She also let her know that finishing the test is what has to be done in order to have the opportunity to do the things that are more satisfactory and imaginative during the school day. Daisy seemed to understand this. She said that she thought the tests might not be so daunting if she were able to spend an hour in the school library before she had to take them. Heather and Daisy agreed that if Daisy could have time in the library before the test, she would do her best to make it through the next testing period.

Workaholics in Severe Distress

The students had been working on group projects in their history class. One day, Wesley walked into class angrily muttering to himself about it not being fair that he should get a D because his partners on a project did not do their part or else they did it wrong. He knew he couldn't rely on his partners and should have done all the work himself. He took his seat, but all through the class he told everyone they were stupid and criticized them for not being able to think straight. Heather went over to him and told him he had gotten the highest grade in the class on the math test. She also asked him if he would be willing to help her by working with some of the students who seemed not to understand the material. Wesley was reluctant at first, but in response to Heather's continued praise for his math skills and his hard work, he finally agreed. Later, while the rest of the class was doing their math work, Heather asked Wesley what had happened in the other class. He explained that the school bus was late and that as a result he did not have time to make sure his partners had done their part of the work on their group project. They had to present their project that morning, and they were not ready. One of his partners did not do anything, and the other partner did his part wrong. As a result, their project was a mess, and they all got Ds. It was the first D Wesley had ever received, and he was upset about it. He did not think it was fair. He had worked very hard on his part of the project, and his part was very well done. He added that if he had known that his partners were not going to do their parts correctly, he would have done the whole thing himself. Heather encouraged him to keep up the good work he was doing in all his subjects and told him she would talk to the other teacher. Heather thought back over all these incidents. By not taking the behaviors personally and by remembering that the students were still good people, she had been able to keep herself in a frame of mind where she could think clearly and communicate clearly with all her students.

She also saw how effective it was when she helped students get their motivational needs met—even when they were doing things that might normally get them sent to the principal's office or get them expelled. Process Communication really was a powerful tool to have in her quiver. Many times it seemed like she had a magic wand that she could wave, and the students would cease their disruptive behaviors and get back to what she wanted them to learn in class.

9

Preparing All Students for Standards and Assessments

The era of standards has arrived. The No Child Left Behind Act requires that schools prove that their students are making adequate yearly progress. School systems across the country have developed standards that students in each grade level must meet in order to comply with this law. Teachers are under tremendous pressure for their students to perform well on the tests that measure the attainment of these standards. Not only is school achievement becoming dependent on the results of these tests, but they have become extremely important to the future of the school, its teachers, and its administrators. But how important are these tests to the students? What is the solution to keeping students motivated in school and on task so that they, their teachers, and their schools can meet the standards set for success?

Students who present major behavioral problems to their teachers are usually not worried about how well they will perform on standardized tests. Perhaps they can be "motivated" by threats of not being promoted to the next grade or not graduating if they do poorly on tests. However, these kinds of negative motivation have disadvantages too. According to Jay Smink, the executive director of the National Dropout Prevention Center at Clemson University, 40 percent of students who repeat one grade and 90% of students who repeat two grades drop out of school (J. Smink, personal communication, November 1, 2004). Moreover, these students are just as likely to purposely do poorly on the test as revenge if they are angry with their teacher.

Research has shown that if we want students to truly learn the curriculum so that they can perform well when tested on it, we must find ways to motivate them through the use of effective teaching strategies. In addition, classroom time must be devoted to learning and practicing the skills needed to solidly learn the curriculum. This can be done only if the management of student and classroom behavior takes a minimum amount of the teacher's time and effort. Process Communication offers teachers methods and techniques to maximize the use of classroom time and to motivate and teach each student efficiently and effectively.

STUDENT MOTIVATION

Pulling students into the fabric of the curriculum, making them feel a part of it, capturing their interest, and finding out what gets them excited are the first steps in getting students to achieve in school, especially those students who have had a history of noninvolvement in academic endeavors. In researching methods for effective teaching, Burden and Byrd (2003) found that motivation plays a major part in student achievement. "If you can motivate students, they are more likely to participate in activities and less likely to get off-task and contribute to disorder" (p. 117). These authors suggest taking time to get to know what interests each student. When the strengths, needs, and interests of the learners are identified, standards-based curricula can incorporate learning and assessment activities that directly address those characteristics.

Once teachers know what motivates students, they can reach their students in a variety of ways. One high school included in a study by Reeves (2004) has the teachers find out each student's "passion." Whether it is cartoons, video games, basketball, or ballet, the teacher then links teaching strategies to these personal interests. This is a school that does not settle for minimum competency on tests but pushes students for goals such as academic recognition and even publication of their work. When Marzano (2003b) studied what worked in effective schools, he found that providing students with specific feedback on their work; involving students in simulations, games, and other activities that are inherently engaging; providing students opportunities to design and work on projects of their own choosing; and training students in motivational dynamics resulted in higher student motivation and achievement. Additionally, providing activities that kept students excited and motivated about learning greatly reduced behavior problems (Marzano, 2003a).

BEHAVIOR AND CLASSROOM MANAGEMENT

Managing the logistics and behaviors of a classroom is another essential part of effective instruction. The correlation between classroom management and student achievement has been emphasized throughout this book. Sagor (2003) reminds us, "If we spend time on behavior, it will reduce the time available for teaching our classes" (p. 118). Edwards (1993) tells us that effective classroom management enhances learning. We see over and over that effective classroom management practices maximize the chances for successful teaching and learning to take place. In fact, classroom management is "one of the most important foundations of good instruction" (Emmer, Evertson, Clements, & Worsham, 1997, p. xi). Obviously, if teachers spend less time addressing behavioral and classroom management problems, more time will be spent on academic material, and the possibilities for higher student achievement are maximized.

This is evident in a meta-analysis of more than one hundred studies done by Marzano (2003a). The studies showed that when effective classroom management techniques were employed, students demonstrated a 20 percent increase in academic achievement. Research supports the conclusion that teachers who are effective classroom managers have students who demonstrate more positive student achievement (Brophy & Evertson, 1976; Marzano, 2003a). The relationship between classroom management and student achievement is clear.

STRATEGIES THAT ENGAGE STUDENTS IN LEARNING

"With calls for accountability coming down from all sides, teachers have an extrinsic motivation for collecting compelling and credible evaluative data to illustrate their instructional effectiveness" (Popham, 2001, p. 127). In their book *Succeeding with Standards*, Carr and Harris (2001) emphasize that attaining standards that have been developed for students can be addressed through the practices and approaches that teachers employ. Therefore, it appears that a major component of effective teaching is the instructional strategies teachers select to convey the curriculum and help students reach identified standards. In order for students to be engaged enough in the academic activities that take place in school and to demonstrate essential progress, teacher practices and strategies must be the focus.

Because effective schools are now defined as those that make adequate yearly progress, it is imperative that teachers become well versed in the strategies used in schools that have continued to reach this goal. What are the components of these effective schools? What is effective teaching?

Many school districts are working to improve the achievement of their students by adapting the Baldrige Education Criteria for Performance Excellence (Baldrige National Quality Program, 2004). They are embarking on an ambitious journey of continuous improvement in student achievement by subscribing to the concepts of learner-centered education. High standards are set for all students, and progress against these standards is measured early and continuously. By focusing on student achievement, they collect data that help them develop an action plan to meet the ever-changing needs of their stakeholders. Subsequently, they create a learning environment based on these data that provides the time and support that each individual student needs to learn.

The requirements, expectations, and preferences of students and stakeholders are key components of setting goals and selecting methods for delivering instruction. Teachers are challenged to develop ways to "attract, satisfy and retain students and stakeholders" (Baldrige National Quality Program, 2004, p. 21). Educators need to be able to tailor learning experiences to individual needs and learning styles. They understand that students learn in different ways and at different rates and consequently need to constantly search for alternative ways to enhance learning. They use a wide range of techniques, materials, and experiences to engage student's interest. In order for students to learn effectively, the students themselves need to be highly engaged not only in the curriculum but also in the data collection itself.

Using the concepts of the Process Communication Model® is a powerful way to support the student, stakeholder, and market focus category of the Baldrige criteria. Process Communication provides methods for promptly meeting student needs and encourages teachers to use innovative, active, and student-centered methods to involve students not only in their own learning but in their own data collection as well. In addition, it focuses on communication skills that help educators efficiently and effectively collect crucial data from parents, staff, and community members.

Schmoker (2001) conducted research and documented strategies used in schools that had shown dramatic improvement in test scores. He examined practices used by teachers in schools that had students of low socioeconomic status, mixed demographics, and a history of low performance. Schmoker's research demonstrates some important components of effective teaching and learning similar to those of the Baldrige program. He also found that the keys to improvement were to combine data analysis, goal setting based on this analysis, and opportunities for teachers to collaborate to develop and share the most interesting and effective ways to address these goals.

Interestingly, what he learned was that rather than spending hours on test preparation by simulating test items, teachers in high-achieving schools employed teaching strategies that had a history of producing overall success. These teachers continually linked the identified goals and standards with specific strategies for teaching the material. One school cited in the study produced higher test results across the board and improved in all areas, putting this school on the "most improved" list in its state. Other schools in the study reported similar results. What were some of the strategies these teachers used?

They found that teaching techniques such as using music and raps as a learning tool to memorize mathematical and language-related rules, hands-on mapmaking activities, and breaking down writing tasks into manageable parts resulted in higher student achievement.

Other school systems with similar test results used real-life societal problems to set up student investigation and analysis in chemistry, allowed students to select a product of their own choosing that represented a solution to a governmental issue, used simulations and role playing to involve students, and made use of student presentations as a way of instructing and learning. These types of learning activities not only held the students to the high standards that the school system identified but also required them to utilize higher-order thinking, problem solving, and application skills (Schmoker, 2001). Studies conducted by Marzano (2003b) indicate that among the most effective teaching strategies are nonlinguistic representations, including pictures to demonstrate content, acting, making physical models, and using mental imagery. In addition, cooperative learning was seen as a successful learning model. Danielson (2002) found that in order to enhance student achievement, meaningful participation in the business world and field trips were significant factors. She also found that students who have opportunities for helping to establish the classroom guidelines, work with younger students, and participate in helping their teachers (i.e., serving as lab assistants) tended to do better in school.

Practices and strategies that teachers employ are crucial to the attainment of standards that have been developed for students (Carr & Harris, 2001). Successful educators recommend such strategies as collaboration in groups, students teaching other students, pursuing understanding through projects, and codesigning learning activities. They suggest using a variety of learning opportunities, including working in pairs, small groups, large groups, and independently. Reeves (2004) recommends combining math and art to help students remember shapes. He also pointed out that displaying exemplary student work in all subjects in the halls of the school keeps students motivated to perform well. Sagor (2003) suggests that for test preparation, the standards on which student will be evaluated be embedded into problem-based learning and other authentic instructional approaches rather than having the students work on simulated high-stakes test questions.

EFFECTIVE INSTRUCTION AND PROCESS COMMUNICATION MODEL®

The ability to identify students' personality types can greatly assist teachers in selecting instructional methods that appeal to students, keep them out of distressful situations, and help them do their best work. Using strategies and activities that appeal to each personality type and that help students stay motivated and on task will naturally lead to higher achievement.

Although Workaholics and Persisters tend to perform well on standardized tests, these two types make up only 35 percent of the school population (Kahler, 1982). Of course, other types are capable of doing well on these tests if motivated and prepared properly. However, when students are in distress from events that occurred either at home or at school, they are not in the best frame of mind to learn, achieve, and perform well on tests. What about the Reactor who desperately wants to please and do well but, when under pressure, makes seemingly small but tragic mistakes, such as skipping a row on the answer sheet and filling in the answers in the wrong places? It can be frustrating to teachers when their Promoter students, who they know are smart and have mastered the material, decide not to buy into the importance of the tests and don't put forth any effort. Preparing for and taking tests that involve sitting for long periods of time, reading, and selecting the right answer can easily

become boring for Rebels, who would rather do something they consider more interesting. Perhaps the most frustrating to teachers is the Dreamer student, who has proven to be so bright and insightful but who can't seem to make a selection from the multiple-choice answers provided or who doesn't finish the test.

As part of the Process Communication Model®, Kahler (1982) has identified motivators for each personality type (see chapter 4). By knowing the types of students in their classrooms, teachers can offer opportunities for each student to become involved in the curriculum through the lens of their own motivational needs. Teachers can select from a variety of proven methodologies that they know will produce the best results with their particular students.

For example, using the knowledge that Promoters and Rebels respond well to being in leadership and center stage roles, do best with hands-on learning tasks, require activities that they consider exciting and fun, and need to move around, teachers can make sure that these types of activities are incorporated into the school day and plan accordingly. This is especially important preceding situations where the students will be required to be seated for prolonged periods of time, such as during standardized testing. Some of the strategies used by educational teams in schools that have been recognized as effective are those that have great appeal to Rebels and Promoters, such as games, cooperative learning, hands-on building of models, role playing, and the use of music and art to learn concepts and memorize material.

The needs of Dreamers, who perform their best when given some solitude, external structure, and projects to deeply investigate, can be incorporated into many aspects of the curriculum. Effective teaching strategies, such as breaking down tasks into manageable parts, allowing students to select and design their own projects, incorporating mental imagery, and using nonlinguistic representations such as pictures to support academic content can help Dreamers achieve in the classroom.

Teachers who realize that their Reactor students are motivated by positive interactive relationships, reassurance, and praise for their personal worth and a safe environment in which to work can easily provide these situations and help the Reactor students be psychologically prepared to do their best. Activities such as helping the teacher as well as other students, involving them in collaborative group projects, and working in pairs make learning appealing to Reactors and provide them opportunities to feel worthwhile.

Workaholic and Persister students do their best work when given recognition for their effort and accomplishments. Posting their exemplary products and making sure that they receive other forms of academic recognition, such as publishing their writing, fulfills their need to be acknowledged for their hard work. Providing them with feedback, as well as allowing them to design and work on their own projects, helps them extend their knowledge and keeps them motivated.

Shiogi (2004) conducted a study in which she investigated the effect of lesson planning on motivation and achievement. Her goal was to "increase the equity of accessibility to the curriculum" (p. 46) for all personality types without lessening the rigor of the curriculum. She included learning activities such as guest speakers, technology, individual inquiry, and group work. She discovered that when she incorporated at least one element in each lesson plan that addressed the motivational need(s) of each of the six personality types, motivation and grades improved for all types.

It is evident that when teachers use their knowledge of the personalities and preferences of their students, student motivation increases, behavior improves, and achievement is higher. For our difficult-to-reach students, it is especially critical that we tailor our teaching so that these students want to participate and become a part of our learning environment. Including the concepts of Process Communication to embed strategies that help students achieve identified standards can and does lead to higher student achievement.

References

American Psychiatric Association. (1994). *Diagnostic and statistical manual of mental disorders* (4th ed.). Washington, DC: Author.

Bailey, R. (1998). *An investigation of personality types of adolescents who have been rated by classroom teachers to exhibit inattentive and/or hyperactive-impulsive behaviors.* Unpublished doctoral dissertation, University of Arkansas at Little Rock.

Baldrige Education Criteria for Performance Excellence. (2004). Milwaukee, WI: American Society for Quality.

Baldrige National Quality Program. (2004). Milwaukee, WI: American Society for Quality.

Borg, W. R., & Ascione, F. A. (1982). Classroom management in elementary mainstreaming classrooms. *Journal of Educational Psychology, 74*(1), 85–95.

Brendtro, L. K., Brokenleg, M., & Van Bockern, S. (1998). *Reclaiming youth at risk: Our hope for the future.* Bloomington, IN: National Educational Service.

Brophy, J. E. (1996). *Teaching problem students.* New York: Guilford.

Brophy, J. E., & Evertson, C. M. (1976). *Learning from teaching: A developmental perspective.* Boston: Allyn & Bacon.

Burden, P. R., & Byrd, D. M. (2003). *Methods for effective teaching* (3rd ed.). Boston: Allyn & Bacon.

Canter, L. (1989). Assertive discipline: More than names on the board and marbles in a jar. *Phi Delta Kappan, 71*, 57–61.

Carpenter, S. L., Musy, T. L., & King-Sears, M. E. (1997). Behavior management methods. In D. F. Bradley, Margaret E. King-Sears, & Diane M. Tessier-Switlick (Eds.), *Teaching students in inclusive settings: From theory to practice* (pp. 322–364). Needham Heights, MA: Allyn & Bacon.

Carr, J. F., & Harris, D. E. (2001). *Succeeding with standards: Linking curriculum, assessment, and action planning.* Alexandria, VA: American Society for Curriculum Development.

Cotton, K. (1990). *School improvement series. Closer-up #9: Schoolwide and classroom discipline.* Portland, OR: Northwest Regional Educational Laboratory.

Curwin, R. L., & Mendler, A. N. (1988). *Discipline with dignity.* Alexandria, VA: American Society for Curriculum Development.

Danielson, C. (2002). *Enhancing student achievement: A framework for school improvement.* Alexandria, VA: American Society for Curriculum Development.

Dreikurs, R., Grunwald, B. B., & Pepper, F. C. (1982). *Maintaining sanity in the classroom: Classroom management techniques* (2nd ed.). New York: Harper & Row.

Edwards, C. H. (1993). *Classroom discipline and management.* New York: Macmillan.

Emmer, E. T., Evertson, C. M., Clements, B. S., & Worsham, M. E. (1997). *Classroom management for secondary teachers.* Boston: Allyn & Bacon.

Englert, C. S. (1984). Measuring teacher effectiveness from the teacher's point of view. *Focus on Exceptional Children, 17*(2), 1–14.

Evertson, C. M., Emmer, E. T., Clements, B. S., & Worsham, M. E. (1997). *Classroom management for elementary teachers.* Needham Heights, MA: Allyn & Bacon.

Gilbert, M. (2004). *Communicating effectively: Tools for educational leaders.* Lanham, MD: Scarecrow Education.

Glasser, W. (1990). *The quality school.* New York: Harper & Row.

Jensen, E. *Super Teaching.* San Diego: The Brain Store.

Jensen, E. (1996). *Brain-based learning.* Del Mar, CA: Turning Point Publishing.

Kahler, T. (1978). *Transactional analysis revisited.* Little Rock, AR: Human Development Publications.

Kahler, T. (1982). Process Communication Model®. Little Rock, AR: Kahler Communications.

Kahler, T. (1996). *Process communication model: A contemporary model for organizational development*. Little Rock, AK: Kahler Communications.

Kahler, T. (1997). Process Teaching Model®. Little Rock, AR: Kahler Communications.

Kahler, T. (2000). *The mastery of management* (4th ed.). Little Rock, AR: Kahler Communications.

Kahler, T., & Pauley, J. (1997). Diagnostic criteria for attention-plethora hypoactivity disorder (A.P.H.D.), also known as fun deficit hypoactivity disorder (FDHD). Proceedings of annual meeting, Kahler Communications, Little Rock, AR.

Kohn, A. (1996). *Beyond discipline: From compliance to community*. Alexandria, VA: American Society for Curriculum Development.

Kounin, J. S. (1970). *Discipline and group management in classrooms*. New York: Holt, Rinehart and Winston.

Lefrancois, G. R. (1988). *Psychology for teaching* (6th ed.). Belmont, CA: Wadsworth.

Levin, J., & Nolan, J. F. (1991). *Principles of classroom management: A hierarchical approach*. Englewood Cliffs, NJ: Prentice Hall.

Marzano, R. J. (2003a). *Classroom management that works: Research-based strategies for every teacher*. Alexandria, VA:

Marzano, R. J. (2003b). *What works in schools: Translating research into action*. Alexandria, VA: American Society for Curriculum Development.

Pauley, J. A., Bradley, D. F., & Pauley, J. F. (2002). *Here's how to reach me: Matching instruction to personality types in your classroom*. Baltimore: Brookes Publishing.

Pedulla, J. J. (2003). State-mandated testing: What do teachers think? *Educational Leadership, 61*(3), 42–46.

Popham, W. J. (2001). *The truth about testing: An educator's call to action*. Alexandria, VA: American Society for Curriculum Development.

Reeves, D. B. (2004). *Accountability for learning: How teachers and school leaders can take charge*. Alexandria, VA: American Society for Curriculum Development.

Sagor, R. (2003). *Motivating students and teachers in an era of standards.* Alexandria, VA: American Society for Curriculum Development.

Savage, R. V. (1991). *Discipline for self-control.* Englewood Cliffs, NJ: Prentice Hall.

Schmoker, M. (2001). *The results fieldbook: Practical strategies from dramatically improved schools.* Alexandria, VA: American Society for Curriculum Development.

Sheets, R. H., & Gay, G. (1996, May). Student perceptions of disciplinary conflict in ethnically diverse classrooms. *NASSP Bulletin,* 83–94.

Shiogi, A. (2004). *Does implementing the Process Communication Model in a unit of my teaching affect my students' motivation in my class?* Unpublished master's inquiry, University of California, Los Angeles.

Stage, S. A., & Quiroz, D. R. (1997). A metaanalysis of interventions to decrease disruptive classroom behavior in public education settings. *School Psychology Review, 26*(3), 333–368.

Stronge, J.H. (2002). *Qualities of effective teachers.* Alexandria, VA: American Society for Curriculum Development.

Wubbels, T., Brekelmans, M., van Tartwijk, J., & Admiral, W. (1999). Interpersonal relationships between teachers and students in the classroom. In H. C. Waxman & H. J. Walberg (Eds.), *New directions for teaching practice and research* (pp. 151–170). Berkeley, CA: McCutchan.

Index

academic performance/achievement, ix, 36, 45, 48, 77, 86, 87, 117, 119, 120, 122, 123, 125

accountability, viii, 14, 120

action, perception of, 7, 13

anger, 108

assessment, 117, 120, 121, 123

attention-deficit/hyperactivity disorder (ADHD), 22, 25, 77–82, 87

Baldrige National Quality Program, 120, 121

behavior management methods, traditional, 38–44

behaviors, negative. *See* distress

classroom management models: assertive discipline, 40, 44; behavior modification, 41, 44; brain-based learning, 46; discipline with dignity, 40; Kounin Model, 40, 42, 44; logical consequences, 40, 44; operant conditioning, 40; Process

Communication Model® (PCM), vii, xiv, 42–48, 49, 50–58, 61–75, 86–87, 91–105, 107–16, 118, 121, 123; reality therapy, 40, 44; student–teacher relationships, 46–48

differentiation, 91–105, 121

disabilities, students with, ix, 95, 96, 103

distress: as cause of phase change, 16; early warning behaviors of Dreamers, 12, 67; early warning behaviors of Persisters, 71; early warning behaviors of Promoters, 61, 62, 79; early warning behaviors of Reactors, 47, 73; early warning behaviors of Rebels, 64, 65, 79; early warning behaviors of Workaholics, 69; as indicator of phase, 109; inviting out of, 109; myths that further, 108; severe behaviors of Dreamers, 114–15; severe behaviors of Persisters, 112–13; severe behaviors of Promoters, 113–14; severe